The first time I met Kendra I saw the shine that she speaks of in her book *Born to Shine*. I already knew of her growing business and what a go-getter she is. I had a meeting with her hoping that I might at some point do some business with her. I'm still hoping that comes to pass.

I'm surprised and touched to know that I have been an inspiration in her life. I have to honestly say after meeting her, she has now become an inspiration in mine.

I really think you will enjoy reading her incredible journey in this book, as I have. She mentions she was influenced and impressed by the movie *9 to 5* and working women. But it's obvious that she has worked longer than 9 to 5 to achieve all that she has achieved. That's a 24/7, 365 job and she's doing it very well. Enjoy!

—*Dolly Parton*

Kendra Scott isn't just a jewelry designer or an entrepreneur. She's an example of the power of persistence to everyone she meets. Kendra's story of perseverance and positivity in the face of life's challenges will inspire readers to dream big, work hard, and forge their own path.

—*Mark Cuban*

You may think you know Kendra Scott's life—all sparkle and sunshine. But in this book, she shows us how beautiful we actually become through the ugly crying, the survival, the gut-wrenching suffering, and the wild fierceness of our lives. That's where the magic is. Thank you, Kendra, my fellow anti-perfection warrior!

—*Jen Hatmaker*

BORN TO SHINE

Do Good, Find Your Joy, and Build a Life You Love

KENDRA SCOTT

NEW YORK   NASHVILLE

These are stories from my life and business,
told from my perspective.

I've changed some names and identifying details.

Worthy
Hachette Book Group
1290 Avenue of the Americas, New York, NY 10104
worthypublishing.com
twitter.com/worthypub

First Edition: September 2022

Worthy is a division of Hachette Book Group, Inc.

The Worthy name and logo are trademarks of Hachette Book Group, Inc.

The publisher is not responsible for websites (or their content) that are not owned by the publisher.

The Hachette Speakers Bureau provides a wide range of authors for speaking events. To find out more, go to www.hachettespeakersbureau.com or call (866) 376-6591.

LCCN: 2022939617

Interior book design by Timothy Shaner, NightandDayDesign.biz

ISBNs: 9781546002321 (hardcover), 9781546002741 (ebook), 9781668610961 (audio)

Printed in the United States of America

LSC-C

Printing 1, 2022

For you: may you shine your light as bright as you can.

As my idol Dolly Parton likes to say,
"if you want the rainbow, you gotta
put up with the rain."

Words to live by.

CONTENTS

Introduction

I'm an optimist to my core: my friends have joked that hanging out with me is like being around a Disney princess who has birds landing on her fingertips to sing her a song. They're wrong about the princess part—I'm Midwestern born, and Texas has been my home for thirty years—but I *am* one of those people who wakes up happy, who sees the best in everything and everyone. I live in the same reality we all do—where bad things happen to good people, where dreams are deferred or crushed altogether, where climbing to a dizzying height means risking a painful fall—I just refuse to let the *worst* of reality become my *entire* reality. Toxic Positivity is forcing a silver lining and denying the reality of the storm: it's not just unhelpful, it's harmful. Optimism, to me, is believing that whatever is in this moment . . . is not forever. It's knowing that there is still possibility and promise in the future, even when the present is messy or painful or downright terrible.

Nature is the original optimist, and she gives us endless examples of promise and renewal and reinvention. My company—Kendra Scott—is known for creating beautiful and affordable jewelry, often with natural gemstones. Gemstones have an undeniable natural beauty that has captivated humanity for time immemorial; we've imbued them with meaning, with powers, we've valued them spiritually and materially.

One of our most popular stones is a form of quartz that dazzles like glitter, catching the light in a million different ways without ever being faceted. It can be cut to form earrings or pendants and dyed to nearly any color in the rainbow, and in any setting or shade, they would dazzle you even in a case filled with diamonds. But quartz—like any other gemstone, like *diamonds*, even—does not start out beautiful. To create these quartz formations, mineralized water evaporates on the surface of a plain old rock, and with the right combination of ingredients, time, pressure, and space . . . we get immense beauty.

Each gem is a product of its environment, a reflection on what came before it. Amethyst is formed in basalt, a rock created by volcanic lava. In the icy waters of Lake Superior, quartz can appear in earth-toned agates, striped with the history of the glaciers that formed the Great Lakes. Quartz formations can be found in old quarries and abandoned mines, a glittering reminder of the persistence of the natural world, who renews and reinvents herself over and over again.

Maybe this is what drew me to these elements in my work, that the stones I formed into necklaces and earrings for my friends, my neighbors, and now for millions of women worldwide reflect the same tenacity and perseverance as the people who treasure them. Often, the rarest of gems are more valued for what makes them different; an imperfection that cannot be replicated suddenly makes them even more special. What if we saw ourselves this way? Each other? What if we looked at our own lives and saw the flaws and cracks and imperfections as features wholly unique to us, assets that increased our value, that make us truly one of a kind.

Gemstones do not have to be rare to be beautiful or valued; quartz makes up a large percentage of our Earth's crust and still we marvel at the way it catches and refracts light, how something so luminous could grow in a place the light never touches. By the time they reach us, we see only the finished product; these naturally beautiful objects don't reveal the immense amount of effort it took to form something so effortlessly beautiful.

You do not need to be perfect to be valued, you do not need to shine for anyone but yourself.

In 2002, I started Kendra Scott in the spare bedroom of my house during my baby's naptime. I started with the $500 I had to spare, and now I stand at the helm of a company valued at over a billion dollars. When you create shiny, beautiful things for a living, the assumption is that your life is also shiny and beautiful. And while my life at times certainly has been shiny and beautiful, it has also been painful and sharp. There is no level of success that can smooth all the edges for you, and I have felt deep cuts over the years. Haven't we all? A guarantee of life is that the unpredictable pendulum can swing any which way, whenever it wants, that over and over again we will need to excavate our own selves and each other from the darkness.

Maybe that's where you are now, trying to make sense of the shadows and find the way up. And if you are, hear me: you do not need to be perfect to be valued, you do not need to shine for anyone but yourself. Gems and stones are formed by a series of seemingly improbable events: the right elements finding their way to each other in the exact right place, and given time, pressure, and space to make something new in the darkness. We live in a culture with plenty of pressure, but little time and space, and it's no wonder so many people feel as though they are imploding under the weight of the world. Pressure without time and space is just extra weight in an overburdened world. Time—patience, persistence—is a requirement for any kind of growth. These treasures grow in cracks and fissures, in spaces where beauty is hard to find. They don't do it for us—they're not sentient, for goodness' sake—but they form themselves into something beautiful, regardless of whether they'll ever be pulled from the darkness to catch the light.

Is this why we've worn them for millennia? Because they signal to us something that we hope to embody? Do they remind us that our own selves are worth developing and appreciating, even if there is nobody around to appreciate it but us? To live a full life, we must have all of the fundamental elements: joy, love, grief, despair, peace. Some of those are shinier and prettier than the others, but all of them are necessary elements for growing something beautiful, something meaningful. This possibility is within all of us—within everyone in our lives, even when we don't see it—and it's our job not just to shine ourselves but to find the shine in others, too.

Wherever you are, wherever you come from, I believe in my heart and soul that you are here for a reason, that you have immense and innate value, that you—a one-of-a-kind gem that could never be replicated—were born to shine.

Kendra

In the Rough

I'm the person my friends and family count on to see the silver lining and throw on a light switch when they're in darkness. But by the winter of 2021, I hadn't been myself for months. I was hollowed out and exhausted, my own personal crises compounded by the pandemic that was wreaking destruction across our planet. We'd temporarily closed over 100 stores and furloughed thousands of staff, stopped executive pay altogether, and pivoted the business so many times the room always felt like it was spinning. No matter what we did, it would never be enough to ease the pain that we saw across the world and in our communities. Twenty years into this business, we'd already weathered and survived one economic collapse and I'd survived divorce . . . but I'd never had my business, my personal life, and the entire world fall apart all at once. My father—my rock—had two heart attacks that nearly killed him, and I had dragged his fiercely independent ass from Wisconsin to Texas so I could do my best to take care of him the way he did for me for so many years. After almost thirty years, we were once again under the same roof, and while *I* loved it, he was unaccustomed to letting anyone— let alone his baby—care for him. I woke up every day with my chest in a tight knot, hoping that down the hall, he would also open his eyes. I went to sleep praying that his beautiful heart would heal. There were too many things that I couldn't fix, too many dark clouds that refused to glimmer for me. Turning on the TV or scrolling through the news, the pain of the entire world was at my fingertips, and it took every tool in my power to keep myself from spiraling out of control.

This is not the kind of thing you share on Instagram, or the kind of thing that gets you a magazine cover or a podcast interview. So, I don't share it. Over the past twenty years, I've built a hobby and an idea into a billion-dollar brand. The necklaces I once made in my spare bedroom are now gift items for new moms, graduates, girlfriends, wives, brides walking down the aisle, and bridesmaids standing beside her at the altar. As I'm writing this book, I'm on a big network TV show, and I've done it all with a big, genuine smile on my face and in my heart. Nobody could guess that at the height of my career, I'm at a deep, personal low.

Every mother makes it a point to make sure that her kids don't worry about her, and I'm no exception. My youngest, Grey, is seven years old, but even my oldest boys Cade (nineteen) and Beck (seventeen) see me as their Wonder Woman. I've always been their fixer, their rock. So I do my best to put on a smile and keep our traditions going even when things feel like they're falling apart. Colorado has always been my happy place: the quiet and the solitude agree with me, and we're lucky to have a place to spend time with our extended family and friends. We've hosted birthdays and holidays and welcomed new years, filled our dining table with food and happy faces. But this winter trip was smaller and quieter, a reflection of the past year and of the memories I still associated with this mountain. It was just me, my sons, and our dogs. Gracie is young and wild, a big fluffy puppy who is filled with joy and energy. Duke is my big lug, eighty-five pounds of fluff and love who tolerates Gracie but really just wants me all to himself. So to clear my mind and give Duke some one-on-one time, I took him for a walk after dinner. We'd drop by the lodge to see if a few minutes by a warm fire and some socially distanced socialization could lift my spirits, and then I'd come back and rally the boys for an epic Ping-Pong match or Uno battle before bedtime. Duke walked patiently beside me while I called my friend Kelly and wept over everything that I couldn't fix. She knew the details of the past year, but I'd held my feelings as close to the vest as possible, and now there was no keeping them in.

In my mind, I'd created a gallery of critics both real and imaginary, people who were comparing me against my peers, my competitors, my friends, the version of me they thought I should be. Their voices were so loud that it distorted my reality, made everything in my path seem worse than it is. I know from my work with therapists and coaches that I can stop these thoughts, examine them, and swipe them away once I've determined they are just thoughts and not facts . . . but that's *hard*, and sometimes, you just need to call someone and cry it out. One of Kelly's gifts is that she can sit with anything—even a hysterical phone call late on a Sunday night. She listened to me pour it all out, and Duke and I walked and walked, the snow crunching under our feet. Duke and I know each other so well that he might well be the love of my life: he's seen me through so much over the past years that he's not *just* a dog, he's pretty much my life partner at this point. He's been a constant companion since the moment he arrived in my life, when I was broken and grieving the loss of my last and final pregnancy. It would take weeks for my body and my heart to catch up with the reality of what we'd lost, and I was aching inside and out, lying in bed crying for the person I'd hoped to bring into this world, for my sons who were so excited to meet their new sibling. I was red-faced and greasy-haired, and Duke crawled into my arms like he knew that a nine-week-old puppy who just wanted to love me was exactly what I needed in that moment. He licked away my tears and fell asleep on my chest, and we formed a bond that cannot be broken. Where I go, Duke goes. He loves long walks, snuggling close to me while we walk the winding mountain roads, protecting me from dangers that are real (mountain lions) and imagined (sorry to every man on a bike who has ever gotten too close to us).

The obsession is mutual, so when he lost his footing on the road we'd walked together a thousand times, when he slipped over the edge and down out of my sight, I didn't even think twice: I followed him.

"Kelly? One second—Duke just fell." I slipped my phone into my pocket and stepped off the road, where Duke had just disappeared from my view. The mountains were frosted with a thick blanket of glittering snow that concealed the landscape beneath. In the summer months, it's obvious that just off this road is a deep and rocky gulch, but on a wintry night it looks like nothing. Its depth is swallowed up in the darkness. Nothing to worry about, unless you're a big, goofy dog who has lost his footing. I could hear Duke whimpering just out of sight, and I needed to get to him. Reaching out to feel for his collar, I slipped, and the mountain seemed to give way beneath me.

It was hard to tell how far down I'd gone until I looked up; the twinkle lights from the towering lodge I had just walked by were completely gone, and the only lights I could see were the brilliant stars against the Colorado night sky. The sounds of the happy people and their happy families— the families I had just waved hello to on my walk—were gone entirely. I was alone. It was almost too much of a metaphor to be true, but the best ones are: *a woman who looks like she's on top of the world is actually . . . stuck in a deep, deep gulch!* I let myself laugh about it, and I couldn't wait to tell Kelly and hear her bright laughter when I told her I had fallen down a damn mountainside trying to rescue this dog. Duke, by the way, was fine. He was overjoyed to see me, even with snow caked to my leggings and my hair matted and wet with snow. I patted my pockets, but my phone was gone. *Oh, man.* I thought. *Kelly will love that.* I use my Apple watch to ping my phone so often that it's become a running joke: *Oh, Kendra didn't answer? Call again, it'll help her find her phone!* It didn't work. My phone was gone, so all I could do was try to figure out how to get out of there.

Falling down is much easier than climbing up (again, could the metaphors be any more apt?). From the road, the gulch looked more like a small ravine. But down there, I felt like I was about to free solo a rock face. I hike often, but the winter boots I was wearing were more style than survival, and I couldn't get my footing. Duke couldn't either, and my amusement at our situation quickly dissolved. *Did I tell the boys where I was walking? Did I even tell them we went for a walk? Will anyone even find me down here?* I screamed. For help, from anyone, anyone at all. Across the road was a side entrance to the lodge, and I prayed for someone to come out for a cigarette or to hail a ride home. I screamed again, and felt my voice absorbing and dissolving into the thick snow that surrounded us. I wasn't dressed for an episode of *Alone*; I was dressed for a walk with my dog and a possible drink at the bar should a handsome stranger cross my path like the Hallmark movie plot that I deserve! But there were no handsome strangers, and with every step, my legs sank deeper into the snow like those nightmares where you know you need to run but can't. There was no way out of it. I became what I feared I had been those past few months: alone.

I don't know how much time passed, but my hands and feet were turning to ice, and my teeth were chattering in my head. I screamed and screamed and screamed, until my throat was raw and my voice was a thin cry in the thin mountain air. Duke stayed close to me, offering me his warmth, crying alongside me. *Are we going to die down here? Will my kids have to read punny headlines about my death?*

GLASS CLIFF?? SUCCESSFUL
BUSINESSWOMAN TAKES A FALL.

DOWNHILL, FAST: KENDRA SCOTT
DIES IN WALKING ACCIDENT

ALL THE WAY DOWN: WOMAN DIES
IN FREAK FALL!!

It would have been funny if there hadn't been an element
of truth to it. I know that one of our favorite national pas-
times is to critique women, to resent their successes and to
celebrate their declines. Our pop culture landscape is littered
with women who got a little too close to the sun, and headlines have made a field day out of female CEOs misstepping
or stepping down for characteristics that are celebrated in
our male counterparts: pushing employees too hard, being
unlikeable. And while I'm not condoning bad behavior for
any executive, it's undeniable that women in power are held
to standards that would never apply to men. Has anyone told
Jeff Bezos that he should smile more?

Hypothermia doesn't feel like you imagine it might: it
isn't chattering teeth and a beard made of frost. While you're
in imminent danger—right at the precipice of death—all of
that stops, and your mind slows along with your breath and
your heart rate. The fear is replaced with calm, the shivers
stop, and you want to drift off to a nice, warm nap.

At this point, I *needed* a nap, didn't I? Wouldn't it feel nice
to just fall asleep and wake up in the new year? Beneath me,

the snow was an inviting cushion. Above me, the stars shone against the inky black of the night sky. And though I knew I should get up, I started to close my eyes . . . maybe, if I just got some rest, I'd wake up and everything would feel better.

Somewhere above me, Cade and Beck were looking for me, bundled up against the cold and racing through the streets above me, calling my name. Back in Texas, Kelly waited for me to call her back. She figured I had hung up or the call had been dropped, but when I didn't call back or answer her call, her Spidey senses tingled. *That's not like Kendra.* She called Cade, my oldest, and asked if I was home.

"Cade," she said, "this is probably crazy, but you should go look for her. She should be home by now." Cade went right to the lodge with Beck, calling a friend to stay with Grey, who was fast asleep. They expected to find me in front of the fire with Duke. They called my phone—no answer—and then they started to worry. They know that I'll take their calls even if I'm in a board meeting, but now my phone was going to voicemail. Nobody they saw on the street had any memory of a woman walking a giant sheep dog.

It was Beck who first heard Duke barking, but when they saw my tracks leading off the road, they both tumbled down in search of me. They found me laying down in the snow, gasping for air, and stripped off their own jackets and threw them around me. Cade, who recently finished his Wilderness Medical Training, rubbed my throat to help ease my breathing, and he and Beck screamed in unison, loud and frantic, until someone heard them. I wouldn't remember any of this, not even being placed on a gurney and reeled up the mountainside by a fire truck like a giant fish. I wouldn't remember being taken to the hospital, where they slowly warmed my body from the dangerously low internal temperature of 89 degrees.

What I would remember is my beautiful boys appearing above me and the last thought to ring through my mind: *I'm not alone. I'm alive. And I'm going to really live.*

I thought I *had* been living. I'd checked off every box on my many to-do lists. I had deep, meaningful friendships and three healthy kids. But I was spread too thin and doing too much, and no matter what the numbers or the magazine articles said, I wondered if I was even doing a good job. I had become addicted to being the helper, to being the person who could solve the problems for my family, my friends, my business. The more people who relied on me, the harder it became to acknowledge the weight of my own personal issues. I could scream until I was hoarse when my physical safety was in jeopardy, so why couldn't I scream for help when it felt like my emotional world was caving in? Well, because when the whole world is suffering, it's hard to feel like your own struggle counts.

I'm tired of women pretending like their work is effortless, their success a fluke, that the success of another woman is a ding against them instead of a point for all of us.

I'm out of that gulch—literally and figuratively—and I know that someday, I could fall back in. And when that happens, I *have* to ask for help. The people who love me came running to the rescue. They heard me when nobody else did, and they'd do it again. I never want to forget that, and I want to keep my own ear trained to hear the cries for help around me. It isn't easy, any of this. It isn't easy even for the women you know who look like they have it all together, who make it to meetings on time and never seem to forget their friends' anniversaries and who throw themed birthday parties for their dogs.

We often assume that we know what other people are going through: we judge each other on appearances and reputations, we resent the rise and celebrate the fall. We often, too, present the best version of ourselves: we edit out the flaws and pretend like we've got it all together. And I don't know about you, but I'm *tired* of it. I'm tired of women pretending like their work is effortless, their success a fluke, that the success of another woman is a ding against them instead of a point for *all* of us. I'm tired of a world where we pretend like the fall never happened and the climb was a breeze. That sleight of hand doesn't serve us, and it doesn't serve anyone else either.

Here's the promise I'd like to see us make for one another: that when we're down, we'll reach out for help. That when we're up, we'll reach back and offer a hand.

Proud to Be a Coal Miner's Granddaughter

*B*efore any brand or business, before any yellow bags or storefront displays, Kendra Scott was just a girl who loved fashion. I did not come from a particularly fashionable city—I had never been to Paris, New York, Milan—but I grew up in the orbit of one of the most fashionable women I have ever known, my dad's sister, Jo Ann.

Aunt Jo Ann was a fashion director at a big department store in big-city Milwaukee, and she absolutely ruined me from a young age! Jo Ann flew to New York for Fashion Week and on regular buying trips to scout the trends that would become the wardrobes of the most fashionable women in Wisconsin. She was tall and elegant and always dressed to the nines, even when she was sitting in my grandparents' dining room for Thanksgiving dinner. Jo Ann's daughter, Kelly, was six years older than me but treated me like we were peers.

When I visited them at their apartment on Wahl Avenue in Milwaukee, it felt like visiting a castle: they lived on the top floor of a converted mansion with dormer windows and a fireplace in every room. Jo Ann got ready at a vanity with gold filigree brushes and huge Venetian mirrors, and she let Kelly and me spend entire days in her expansive closet, where designer clothes hung in rainbow order on padded hangers. Jo Ann would zip us into her shoulder-padded cocktail dresses, help us select the right bag to go with the kitten heels on which we were struggling to balance, and ask for our suggestions on what she should wear to work the next day. I'd sit on the floor in Jo Ann's gorgeous living room, with its twelve-foot ceiling, and she'd close the floor-length drapes and dim the lights to show me slides of the fashion shows she'd attended. She'd click through photos of women in gorgeous outfits in cities I'd never heard of and ask me to look for patterns: what colors did I keep seeing? What styles? I'd nervously reply with *I see lots of blues* or *I saw pleats three times* and she'd nod in excitement. She was teaching me trend forecasting and showing me a world I longed to be a part of, where beauty and style were in the details most people wouldn't have even noticed.

I imagined myself growing up to be just like Jo Ann, surrounded by beauty and style at work and at home, making a life of my own on my own, just like she did. She'd grown up in Kenosha, and now she flew around the world to go to fashion shows for brands like Oscar de la Renta, Carolina Herrera . . . all the names I recognized from my *People* magazines and saw hanging in her closet. The only Oscar in Kenosha was Oscar Meyer. Someday, I knew, I'd be working in fashion. I'd work my way up from whatever starting point I could find. And as it turns out, that starting point was not quite as glamorous as I'd hoped. It meant putting on a big cartoon bear costume that smelled like feet and sweat and old pizza, and dancing to the oldies as one of the mascots for the Kenosha Twins, our town's minor league baseball team.

My friends and I spent plenty of summer nights at the field, not because we liked baseball but because the players were so cute. We'd sip our Diet Coke and flip our teased hair and wonder if the first baseman was looking at us. Of course, he wasn't, because we were a gaggle of awkward teenage girls, but every warm summer night spent at the field shimmered with possibility. One night, I asked the guy at the box office if they were hiring, and to my absolute shock, he said yes, and I could start at the next home game. I sat through the game vibrating with excitement: I had a job! I didn't know what job it would be, but I had one. Maybe I'd be filling those little paper bags with cheap popcorn dyed with yellow butter flavor, or put on a little baseball outfit and hand the players their bats? I showed up to my first day in an oversized T-shirt, pegged jeans, and my spanking new Reeboks, ready to work. I was not, however, ready to step into a bear costume that still felt damp from the sweat of whatever boy had worn it last. But it didn't matter. I had work to do.

The work meant hyping up the crowd by dancing like a fool to oldies songs: I made up my own dance routines or copied Paula Abdul moves I remembered from MTV. At the seventh inning stretch, I created an interpretive dance to go with "Take Me Out to the Ballgame," and by the time the game wrapped, I could finally take off the giant fiberglass bear head, step out of that furry jumpsuit, and collect my pay: $10 in cold, hard cash. Game after game, I stepped into that bear costume and watched the crowd through the black screens of the bear's eyes. I loved seeing people laugh and dance along. Win or lose, I was a part of something bigger than myself. I had the power—in this reeking costume that seriously needed to be disinfected—to make people smile, to bring happiness to their day.

But baseball in the Midwest stops when the snow falls, and when the season ended, I put on my frostiest lipstick and walked myself down to Southport Rigging in downtown Kenosha. Southport Rigging was *the* skateboard shop—still is, all these years later—where the cute skater boys came in looking for trucks and decks and wheels and bearings. I had never been on a skateboard and thought that trucks were a kind of automobile. But I dressed the part—in an oversized T-shirt and checkered vans—and asked to talk to the manager. He was in his early twenties and seemed confused to see me standing at the counter with my application filled out in purple ink.

I gave him a firm handshake like my dad had taught me and told him my name was Kendra . . . and I was going to be his new part-time cashier. It wasn't so much an interview as it was an announcement, and it worked. For the princely sum of $3.35 per hour, I spent twenty hours a week unpacking boxes, hanging up T-shirts, and organizing stickers. It was my first fashion job: skater style was *hot* and I knew how to sell a pair of checkered vans or some parachute pants and how to accessorize them. I didn't need to know anything about skateboarding. I was there to help even the kids with no balance look like they belonged at the skate park.

Like all kids, my children have grown up hearing stories about their mom's childhood. They know better than to complain about how "cold" winter in Texas is because they know that Wisconsin isn't "wear a coat today" cold, but "I'm losing feeling in my toes" cold. Kids who grow up in Wisconsin are given a snow shovel the minute they can walk because someone needs to help Dad dig out the car when the winter sky dumps twelve inches of snow overnight. While the rest of the world might define cold according to the temperature where water turns to ice, we know that freezing weather is relatively warm when compared to the below zero days that freeze your tears into icicles on your eyelashes, or the days when the wind chill chaps your cheeks the moment you step outside.

As much as I would like an award for surviving those cold winters (mostly by snuggling up on the couch after school with a pile of magazines and blankets), I grew up knowing that winter for my mother had always been far harder than any winter I'd survived. Now, every parent wants their children to know how good they have it, but the age-old exaggeration "in my day, we walked to school uphill both ways . . . in the snow" isn't far from the truth for my own mother. Mom grew up only five and a half hours from Kenosha, if you're driving the speed limit (and a good forty-five minutes shorter if you drive like my father), but in an entirely different world.

Tamaroa, Illinois, was a town of just a few hundred people, but Mom didn't live in town. She was a farm kid; her family homestead was hundreds of acres tucked back behind a gravel road, a few shabby looking outbuildings, and a small home that didn't have running water. Before you begin to envision *Little House on the Prairie*, remember that this was in the 1960s in America! While other girls of her generation were coming of age on the eve of the sexual revolution, my mother woke up every day to pump water out of a well for her own mother to use for cooking, bathing, and hydrating her nine (that's not a typo!) children.

The farm was a cocoon, a cozy, self-sustaining ecosystem. Grandma Edith and Grandpa Joe canned and pickled the vegetables they grew in the summer, made jams, and filled the cellar with venison (that's deer meat for those of you city folks). Unlike my summers in Kenosha, which I spent lying in my backyard reading fashion magazines and using baby oil to help speed up the tanning process, my mother's parents and siblings spent their summers preparing for the coming winter, making sure that they did all they could to ensure the survival of their family. Their cellar was lined with glass jars of canned tomatoes and beans, raspberry jam, baskets of potatoes—the fruits of the land, stored to last them through a cold winter. At night, my grandfather left the farm to work in the coal mines, coming home at dawn to sleep for a few hours before waking up and starting all over again. Before he fell into bed, bone tired and sore, Grandpa Joe scrubbed his calloused hands with the same water my mother had hauled up to the house that morning.

My mother and her siblings grew up knowing what work looked like. It was sore muscles and cracking skin on your hands; it was a job well done if not well paid. While their father slept, my mother and her eight siblings dressed and ate quietly before walking up the road to a one-room schoolhouse. Their lives mirrored the Loretta Lynn song that became legendary half a generation later but which they could have written together.

> *Yeah, I'm proud to be a coal miner's daughter*
> *I remember well, the well where I drew water*
> *The work we done was hard*
> *At night we'd sleep 'cause we were tired*

Life on the farm was hard, sure, but it was the life they knew. It was the same life that was being lived by all the kids in that same one-room schoolhouse, the same life her parents had lived. It was fully expected that my mother and her siblings would carry on this tradition. As children they understood that when they were married, their parents would carve off a piece of land for each of them to settle with their own family. Together, they'd made an unincorporated village of children, siblings, cousins, and grandchildren. It was a simple life, and a good one. What could be better?

Just a few hundred miles northeast of where my mother was living off the land, my father and his sister were being raised in an apartment in Chicago, where my Grandpa Dick worked as the parts manager for a Chevy-Cadillac dealer and my grandmother sold shoes while her kids were at school. Grandma Irene's job was commission-based—sink or swim— and she was swimming laps in no time. She took immense pride in taking her checks to the bank and watching the deposits add up to a better future for her children. The house in Kenosha was a dream come true: the dealer Grandpa Dick was working for relocated to Wisconsin and invited my grandfather to come along as parts manager. The new job was good money in a much less expensive city, and they spent two years growing their savings and renting a house until they had enough for a three-bedroom, one-and-a-half-bathroom colonial on the corner of Nineteenth Avenue and Washington Road, with a separate bedroom for each of their children and a backyard that begged to be gardened.

The best lessons you learn are the ones
you never realize are being taught to you.

Compared to my mother's home, this modest Midwestern house was a palace, but my dad's parents were hardly royalty. They'd survived the Great Depression, scrimped and saved every penny they could, and never stopped working, even when they had achieved the dream of home ownership. Grandpa Dick applied a fix-it mentality to everything in his life. Every summer he removed the storm windows and scraped and repainted the window frames. Every spring and fall he got on the tallest ladder I'd ever seen and cleaned out the gutters. On weekends, he'd consult the list of slight imperfections he and his bride had noticed and get to work on the remedy. Nail holes were patched, peeling wallpaper was re-glued, and even the garage floor was swept clean. His workdays never really ended, he just shifted his focus after five o'clock from starters and pistons to the kitchen faucet and the garage radio. His workbench was lined with small jars of nails and screws and nuts and bolts—new and used—and there wasn't a thing in his home he wasn't able to fix himself. Neither Grandma Irene or Grandpa Dick had anything beyond a high school education, and neither of them were dummies either. Grandma Irene was an equal partner to her husband, and their shared goal was to make sure that their two children could grow up to do anything they wanted.

While my mother and her siblings were expected to stay on the farm, my father and his sister were encouraged to go, to dream, to let their roots stabilize them but not immobilize them. My dad and his sister grew up aware of the cost of things—not just the price tag on their school clothes but the hours of their parents' work that each item represented. They had what they needed, and they took nothing for granted. So when my father applied to the University of Wisconsin and was accepted, he wasn't expecting his father to write him a check to cover the tuition. But he did, and it was an astounding act of love and generosity. Dad left for Madison knowing that the next few years mattered, that the work he did should honor the work his parents had done to get him to this place. He sent home his papers and report cards, and called every Sunday to let them know what he was learning and how he was doing. And when he was accepted into law school three years later, he was just as shocked when his parents ended their celebration dinner with a check to cover his law degree, including room and board. His sister was just starting college at the University of Wisconsin at Whitewater. Were they *sure* they could afford this? Shouldn't they spend the money on something for themselves—a new car, maybe a vacation? But his father pressed the check back into his son's palm. They had Jo Ann's education covered, too. They didn't want a new car, and they didn't need a vacation. This was the point of all that work: that their children could keep growing, keep going. And my father did. Those roots that my grandparents provided him gave him stability and flexibility, and when he graduated from law school, he moved back into his childhood bedroom to start his law practice in downtown Kenosha. He wasn't embarrassed to return to the nest, and in two years his own practice was stable enough for *him* to have his own place.

The farm that had been my mother's cocoon was ours every summer when we were dropped off for a few weeks with our grandparents. I loved the rumble of the gravel beneath our car wheels and the way my grandmother's face lit up when she came out of the house to meet our car. My grandfather wasn't working in the mines anymore, but the work had taken a toll on him. He was still big and strong to me, but he walked with a slower step and had a cough that seemed to rattle in his chest. From the moment we arrived on the farm, we were farm girls. I would ride the combine in my grandpa's lap and pick big buckets of raspberries to turn into jam. Dinner was the chicken I helped catch and the corn I helped shuck.

"Get him, KendraLee!" Grandpa Joe would cheer while I chased the chickens around the yard. He said my first and middle names as if they were just one word, and it felt like a special code just between the two of us. If Grandma Edith was awake, she was constantly moving, either cleaning up from the last mealtime or preparing for the next one. At the end of the day, their dinner table—worn with the decades of children and grandchildren who had eaten their meals there—would be spread with bowls of delicious food from the land. Mashed potatoes, cream corn, green beans, gravy, homemade corn-bread, pie. They didn't have a lot of money, but what Grandma Edith did in her tiny kitchen with her little oven would be hard for a full culinary team to replicate, and to this day I'd take a farmer's dinner over any five-star restaurant. Before we ate, we bowed our heads beneath the cross that looked over their din-ing room and said grace. Grandma Edith and Grandpa Joe were Bible folks who had trusted in God to help them raise and protect their family, and even if our tummies were rumbling, we knew not to touch our forks until Grandpa said "Amen," when the room would fill with the clatter of silverware, laugh-ter, and conversation. We fell into bed every night exhausted and woke up with the sun. I hold a picture in my mind of my grandfather's strong hands, rough with years of mining and farming, and how he'd laugh at his soft-handed granddaugh-ters when we complained about a chore he'd given us. "What you gotta remember, KendraLee," he'd laugh in his booming voice, "is that work is not a four-letter word."

The best lessons you learn are the ones you never realize are being taught to you, and my parents and grandparents taught me how to work and how to love. We grew up closer geographically to my dad's parents. Grandma Irene and Grandpa Dick were just a few minutes away from us in Keno-sha and were so thrilled to be grandparents that they felt more like an extra set of parents to me. From the age of five, I had my own bedroom at their house, and my favorite snacks were always on hand in the refrigerator. Grandma Irene treated me like a treasured house guest, serving me TV dinners on a tray in front of my favorite shows and running warm bubble baths for me in her pink-tiled bathroom. She was tall and thin, and always—always—dressed in a skirt. It was the eighties, so of course she wore giant glasses to frame her ice-blue eyes. Grandpa Dick loved it when I kept him company in the garage as he changed the oil in Grandma's car or tinkered with one of his many home projects. He looked like a movie star, with a thick head of dark hair grayed at the temples and an impeccable daily uniform of pleated slacks, a cardigan, and spotless shoes. They were long retired by the time I came around, but work was a part of their daily lives, a form of service to their family and to each other. The house they bought when they were just scraping by had been long paid off and was now a place for their children and grandchildren to come for dinner and Christmas and a good cup of coffee. Nothing had ever been promised to them, and like so many people who survived the Depression, they were always ready to make do with less or to go without. They didn't live in fear of losing it all, but they did live with immense appreciation of what they had.

My grandparents were not defined by their work, but their work defined who they were: people with principles and passions, who took seriously their responsibility to contribute to their family and to their community. Grandma Irene wasn't just keeping house, she was taking care of her family and planting the seeds for a different life for her children. Grandpa Joe wasn't just mining coal, he was powering the lights that his future son-in-law studied by just a few hours away. At fourteen, I wasn't passionate about baseball, but I loved making people smile. Working at the skate shop definitely wasn't about my passion for skateboarding, but every time I sent a customer out the door with what they needed to pursue *their* passion, I felt amazing. I felt like more than just a part-time cashier who also cleaned smudges off the windows and folded T-shirts. I felt like a person who had helped make the world better, one skater at a time . . . for minimum wage. It's not just what we do, but why we do it. All four of my grandparents were in a much different financial position than I am today. Of course, they worked for money, to pay the bills, to keep food on the table. But that is not enough to keep you climbing down into a mineshaft or stuck under a car for eight hours a day.

My work is not my purpose, but it powers my purpose.

My work is not my purpose, but it powers my purpose: it has empowered me to create beauty, create jobs, create opportunity, and cultivate a culture where the better we do as a company, the more good we do for the world.

My oldest sons, Cade and Beck, are barely three years apart in age and have grown up alongside my business. Their early childhoods were spent in my offices, napping in pack and plays as babies, coloring on printer paper as toddlers, and finishing their homework or playing board games as little kids. Cade loved to crawl through the office looking for any loose gems or beads. Beck loved to organize materials by color or type, and my employees and I loved having a few moments of quiet so we could have a conference call. My boys have seen this business grow from a spare bedroom to a headquarters in downtown Austin, and they've seen our own world grow along with it. They have always known that they will need to find their own path and earn their own way in this world, that they will not be getting a free ride because they had the luck to be born into this family.

As a kid, I learned that all work was meaningful.

Parenting is filled with moments that your brain knows to remember forever: first steps, first teeth, first days of school. There are some images I can recall with picture-perfect clarity: how I cheered so loudly when Cade took his first steps that he fell on his butt and cried. Cade holding Beck's hand and walking his little brother into his first day of kindergarten in their matching backpacks. And I'll forever treasure the spring day—just after he turned fifteen—that Cade told me he had a job. He didn't just want one, he already had one. He'd done what I did when I was fourteen, though the child labor laws have tightened a bit since the 1980s and he did have to be fifteen and fill out an application. I've lived in Texas for most of my life, but my Midwestern roots run deep and strong. Seeing that famed Midwestern work ethic in a born and bred Texas boy made my heart swell. I was as proud of him as I was the day he was fully potty trained, and any parent can tell you that's a tough moment to beat.

Cade's first job, at Ceasar's Hand Detailing, was washing cars. Ceasar's is in the Tarrytown area of Austin. It's the best carwash in the wealthiest ZIP code in the city, where a parade of Range Rovers and Mercedes and other luxury vehicles roll in weekly to be meticulously cleaned. That summer the average temperature hovered in the low nineties, and five days a week Cade went to work with a cooler for lunch and a giant thermos of water. In a twist of irony, he couldn't yet drive, so I gave him a ride. He vacuumed crumbs from the seats of his sports rivals' cars and wiped the windshields of the kids who sat at his lunch table. He earned tips from women wearing the jewelry his mother designed and got constructive feedback from a neighbor who noticed there were streaks on the rear windshield and asked him to do it over again. A few years later, Beck was working there, too, coming home bone tired and proud of having earned his own way.

That's what they *did*, but what it meant was that they had responsibility and independence. It meant that they were more than just a rich kid getting an allowance—they were their own people, taking charge of their own destiny. That first year, Cade came home every day having sweated clear through his uniform, his shoes and socks soaking wet and left in the entryway.

"How was your day?" I'd ask him, pushing a plate of the dinner he'd missed across the counter and trying to ignore that he smelled as if he'd bathed in air freshener.

"Awesome," he'd reply, smiling in between bites. "It was awesome."

He's exactly right. As a kid, I learned that all work was meaningful, whether it took place in my dad's "fancy" downtown law office or out on the land with my cousins. I knew that it wasn't meant to be easy, and it wouldn't always be fun, but that it was a part of a purposeful life: work is not our life or our identity, but it gives identity and meaning to our lives. There is a lot of messaging out there that disparages the work that makes our world *work*, viral videos that tell people it's not ambitious enough to clock in at a day job that pays your bills, that the only work worth doing is work that is "big" and "audacious." To me, these messages are toxic. They ignore the fact that many people don't have the time, resources, and additional mental space to take on the risks of entrepreneurship, and that—more importantly—the meaning of life is not to drive yourself into the ground but to be present with ourselves and each other. Konstantin Stanislavski said, "There are no small parts, only small actors." There are no small jobs either. The meaning and passion behind our work—whatever that work is—can simply be to give us the capacity to enjoy our lives outside of work. To send our kids to camp, or have movie nights on the couch, or pay the bills that keep the lights on. It is never meaningless, small, or insignificant to care for yourself or the people around you. In fact, it's awesome.

*The meaning of life is not to drive
yourself into the ground but to be present
with ourselves and each other.*

Three

Family First

My mom was happy on the farm, and she was loved. And yet, she was also always a little different from her siblings and her parents. From the moment she could read, and the letters on the page rearranged themselves into words and sentences and entire worlds inside of her mind, she would read anything she could get her hands on. She tore through the small stack of books available at their tiny school, she kept brochures dropped off by wayward door-to-door salesmen, and she wanted more.

It was rare for my mother's family to leave the confines of their little world, but one day my mother was lucky enough to take a day trip with her aunt to the town of Du Quoin, Illinois. Now, Du Quoin is not much larger than Tamaroa, but they did have a shopping center. And it was there, riding an escalator for the first time, that my mother had the realization that there really was life outside of their farm and their family. That the books she loved may be fiction, but they were also representative of a bigger, wider world. I should mention that Du Quoin is home to approximately six thousand people as of the last census, and still, my mother was transfixed and transformed. Here were all these people she'd never seen before, doing things she'd never seen done before. Things like riding a moving staircase or walking into stores lined with outfits of all colors and sizes that were most certainly not homemade hand-me-downs. She was a visitor to another planet, and she longed to go back. She imagined herself as one of those women clicking through the shopping center with perfectly set hair and a handbag that matched her shoes. She saw herself opening a billfold and buying the dress she wanted, not the dress made of potato sacks. She saw a life for herself, and even though it was just an afternoon away with her aunt, she held on to that vision back at the farm. Hauling up the day's water, she remembered the shiny taps in the ladies' restroom. Knotting her frayed shoelaces, she remembered the crisp white sneakers she'd seen in a shop window. And paging through the worn books in her classroom, she smelled the bookstore where she and her aunt had browsed that afternoon. Afternoons away from the farm remained a rare part of her childhood, but every visit to town reinforced this curiosity, this sureness that the path she was born on was not the only path.

My mother was young when she got pregnant by her high school sweetheart. She did what she was supposed to, she got married, and by twenty was the mother of three little girls— my sisters Karla, Diana, and Rhonda. She and her husband had left the farm and moved to Kenosha, Wisconsin, where

Mom worked as a secretary at the Chevy dealership, answering phones and greeting customers and filing all the necessary paperwork for the sales team to close their deals. She was an indispensable member of the team and loved by *everyone*, including the parts manager . . . my Grandpa Dick. Grandpa didn't know he was working with his future daughter-in-law; he just knew that this sunny blonde who kept everyone on their toes was a mother of three and that money had to be tight.

One day by the coffee machine, he let her know that his son just happened to be a lawyer who needed some help getting his practice up and running. He didn't know what the pay was exactly, but he was sure that it would be better than what the dealership could offer. Mom loved her job, but a bigger paycheck would make a big difference. She and my sisters lived in a little three-bedroom house on the edge of Kenosha. Mom couldn't afford a car, so she walked *everywhere*. Her own parents had urged her to come back home. The land was still there; her siblings were still there. In Tamaroa, her daughters could be raised alongside their cousins, aunts, and uncles. It takes a village to raise three children, and she had one waiting for her. She stayed up at night, curled up on the couch in their little rented house, feeling the cold wind sneak through every seam in the walls. But Mom didn't go home. She took the business card my grandpa offered her and called the number on the card. And a few days later, she was walking to downtown Kenosha to interview for a secretary position with an attorney named Ken.

Kenosha, Wisconsin, is a small city on Lake Michigan. It's in the southern part of the state, the halfway point between Milwaukee and Chicago. It has a small-town feel to it, with a downtown lined with historic brick buildings, a lighthouse, all the charming elements you'd expect to see in a Hallmark movie. Which is why it's the perfect scene for the love story I'm about to tell you. This is a story I begged to hear over and over again as a child, and one my own imagination has filled in over the years, surely romanticizing away any sharp edges.

The day of the interview, Mom left my sisters with a neighbor and told them to wish her luck. I imagine her practicing her interview voice in the mirror, leaving extra time for the walk so she wouldn't be late, knowing that the fates of her *and* her girls hung in the balance. I can see her—young, gorgeous, and brave as hell—marching up the street with all of the false confidence she could muster. I love to imagine her walking into that office, dark and scholarly with law books lining the walls and deep leather chairs in the waiting room, and meeting the man who would become my father.

My father, Ken, was six foot three, a big man with a big personality, like a combination of Tom Selleck and Burt Reynolds: tall, dark, and handsome. Mom was fair and small, with flowing blonde hair, bright blue eyes, and the kind of natural beauty that only looked more natural with the light touch of her makeup. Dad was just starting out, and the office was a *mess*. He had legal files piled in the waiting room, and his filing "system" was nearly nonexistent. He'd picked his office for the location—it was across the street from the courthouse—and the minute Mom arrived, he had to leave for a hearing. Would she mind, he asked, just staying put until he got back? It was a little annoying and quite unprofessional, but he was so warm and so sincere that Mom said fine, she could wait.

She didn't exactly *wait*. She spent about two minutes sitting in the chaos of his office before she got to work. When Dad got back, he found that the woman he was *about* to interview had already organized his entire office while he was gone: the piles of paper were in neat files, the filing cabinets were labeled, and for the first time since he'd gotten it, his desk was clear. He was stunned and asked her the only questions he could think of. "Is eighty dollars a week okay?" And "When can you start?" Eighty dollars a week was a windfall to Mom, and she practically floated on her walk home. That paycheck left her with enough money after rent to save up some cash, and in a few months, she bought herself a car: a 1962 Rambler in lime green. It was a clunky sedan with the kind of gearshift she'd learned driving the tractors back in Tamaroa, and it was all hers for just $35 a month. For months, she sat at the secretary's desk at the front of the office, vetting potential clients for the man who would be my father. He trusted her judgment and told her that if a criminal case came in and *she* thought they were guilty, she had the right to tell them that he would not be taking the case. She kept his billing and accounting straight while he drove back and forth between Wisconsin and Illinois for trials and helped build his dream into a real business. At the end of the workday, she'd tidy up her desk, get in her car, and drive back to her little house to relieve the babysitter and make supper for my sisters.

I see a movie montage of all her hard work paying off: signing her name in beautiful cursive on her checks and placing the envelopes in the mailbox downtown, food in her cupboards, and a little extra money to buy a few more blouses to wear with her suit. When my mom and dad fell in love—and no, it didn't take long—he raised her daughters as his own. No longer was my mom rattling down the street in a beater, she was driving a car where all four doors opened and closed without even kicking them. It was a brand-new Camaro, and no, that's not a great car for little kids, but the 1970s were a different time, and they were young and in love and building a life together. I was their last baby, named for my father and the final piece in a collector's set including Rhonda, Diana, and Karla. We became a family of six and settled into a real family home in Kenosha proper. It was a white brick colonial with a mansard roof, built and designed by my parents as their dream house for their dream of a family. It was just a few minutes from my father's parents, who had encouraged him to go as far as he could. Turns out, he could take his dreams as far as he wanted in his hometown.

Growing up, the kind of family you have is the only kind of family you know about, but even if I'd been given a menu of options, I'd have picked being the youngest of four girls. When Mom and Dad brought me home from the hospital, Karla was thirteen, Diana was eleven and a half, and Rhonda was nine. I was their little doll; my parents were sure that I was a perfect baby who slept through the night, but in reality, they'd put my crib in my eleven-year-old sister Diana's room. There wasn't room for a nursery (were those even a thing yet?) and Diana would wake up when I cried and rock me back to sleep. When I was old enough to have my own big-girl bed, I became roommates with my sister Rhonda. We had twin beds and kelly green shag carpeting that she divided with masking tape to keep me on my side. It didn't work, of course, because she was my cool older sister and I really wanted her to play Cabbage Patch dolls with me.

When Karla got to high school, she and her boyfriend would take me everywhere with them, and I mean everywhere. They'd put me in the backseat and drive me out to Crystal Lake, where the local teens partied in the summer. They acted like teen parents: splashing with me in the shallow water, packing a picnic lunch, and stopping at Shirl's Custard Shop on the way home for ice cream. Rhonda as an adult is four foot eleven with feet smaller than my eight-year-old son, but as a kid she was like a little china doll. She used to entertain me by taking me down to the basement, where she'd put on a record, lip-synch, and dance along. I *loved* it, except for the time we both learned the hard way that a toddler can't really sit on a barstool unattended. The long-standing joke in my family is that the fall explains a lot about my personality. Rhonda is a brilliant piano player with an incredible singing voice, and throughout my childhood I watched in awe at her little hands dancing up and down the keys, at the way her voice could grow and stretch to fill a room with feelings I didn't even know how to identify yet. My life, as you can tell, was perfect. I thought I lived in a palace growing up, and why wouldn't I? I had a Strawberry Shortcake doll with all the scented accessories . . . and eventually got to move into "the pink room," with—you guessed it—hot pink shag carpeting and a four-poster bed with a matching desk. Unlike today, where every house is decorated in neutrals, my mom firmly believed that every room should have its own color and personality . . . and coordinating shag carpet. Maybe this is where I got my love for color? My mother's values from growing up on the farm were a part of our daily life. Our basement had a wall of canned goods that we'd picked and preserved ourselves: beans, tomatoes, and jam made from the strawberries we'd pick in the summer. We lived the way my parents had grown up: family first, always. Even with four kids and a busy law firm, we always, always had dinner together at the table at six o'clock.

But the thing about kids is that they grow up, and when Karla left for college when I was just five years old, it felt to me like I was losing a mother. When she called home, I'd cling to the telephone receiver as though I were gripping her neck, and she'd tell me how much she missed me and how many days I'd have to wait until her next visit. When Diana joined her a year later, I thought I would die. I was in first grade, sobbing in the basement bedroom my dad had created for Karla and Diana during their high school years, a "cool" space with lava lamps, bean bag chairs, and yes, of course . . . shag carpeting. Diana was moving in with Karla, not into a dorm but into a trailer near the University of Wisconsin at Whitewater campus. It was maybe an hour and a half from our front door, which might as well have been on another continent. I could *hear* the distance when Karla called, and now Diana would be a voice on the other side of the phone, too. I watched Diana wrap her picture frames in tissue paper, fold her clothes and stuff them into duffle bags, and I let my big, fat tears fall onto the carpet I was laying on.

"Kendra," she said in her sweet voice, "it's okay, I promise. You're going to be okay." She tried to tell me that someday *I* would go to college, that *I* would move out of this house and off on my own. Was she *crazy*? I was never leaving this house! I'd live here until I was an old lady, with Mom and Dad. Diana had to literally shake me off her bellbottom jeans to get into her car, and it felt like I didn't stop crying until she called a few weeks later to tell me she was coming home . . . to pick me up and take me to college for the weekend. I couldn't believe what I was hearing, and when I ran to tell my parents I was going to college next weekend, they looked at me like I had two heads. How many college freshmen come back to their hometown to pick up their kid sister for a weekend in a single wide? They'd made their little trailer cozy and colorful, and sitting on the linoleum counter was a gift bag with my name written on it in bubble letters. Inside were two small Smurf figurines for my bedroom at home . . . and a purple satin UW-Whitewater jacket. I slid it on and knew that I wouldn't take it off unless somebody forced it off my scrawny little arms. I would bathe in it. I would sleep in it. I would never—ever—take it off. I wore it the entire weekend, while the three of us ate pizza and danced and sang in their tiny living room. No matter where they were, I knew, my sisters loved me just the same.

We hardly ever know what moments and memories will become building blocks for who we are.

Four

9 to 5

If you haven't yet seen the iconic film *9 to 5* with Dolly Parton, Jane Fonda, and Lily Tomlin, you should know that there are major spoilers ahead. This is your invitation to set down this book and fire up a movie that is both a time capsule of 1980s fashion and a timeless story about gender parity in the workplace that stands the test of time.

And then, it all changed. I was nine when my parents explained to me that they both loved me, but they didn't love each other, and they were getting a divorce. Our big family now seemed . . . so small. My sisters were far away, and now it was just going to be me, ping-ponging between my mom and dad. Over a million other families in the US went through divorce that year, but as a kid, you're sure it's happening only to you, that yours is the only family fracturing and falling apart, that you're the only kid crying into her pillow so her dad won't hear. When you're nine, you don't know anything about romantic relationships. If you're lucky, you just know that your parents are together and they're in love. You don't know that sometimes two good people don't make a great match, or that time and circumstances can cause people to grow apart. You just know that a wrecking ball has swung through your life and your heart.

My mom had been a mother for over half her life at this point. She'd spent her twenties and thirties taking care of husbands and children and trying to carve out a space for herself in this world. She'd been a Mary Kay beauty consultant and then earned her way to becoming a director, taking what most people thought of as a "side gig" and turning it into a full-on team called Jan's Jewels, who met in the basement my father had converted into a "beauty space" just for their meetings. Every month, the Jewels would convene, crowding around the vanity mirrors my father had hung on the basement walls and gathering at the big table to pass around color swatches and spray fragrance on the inside of their wrists. She was great at it, but after she and my dad divorced, she realized that she needed something new, something hers. It's not particularly easy to launch a new career when you've spent most of your working years doing the unpaid and mostly thankless job of motherhood, but not long after the divorce my mother was offered a really good job—a career-making job—and she took it. This was the eighties, and career-building opportunities for women with a high school education didn't come along every day. The downside: the job was in Chicago, a nearly two-hour drive from Kenosha. That's a hell of a commute, and we were many decades away from Zoom meetings and laptops, so she decided to move to Chicago, and we all decided I should stay in Kenosha with my dad.

I'm sure, having gone through my own divorces and raising my own children, that it wasn't that simple for her, and that the decision to leave me was agonizing. I won't pretend that I understood it at the time. I was just a kid, and her absence echoed inside of me. It wasn't that far, but it felt like an ocean away, even though she called regularly and I got to go down and visit some weekends. My dad assumed primary custody—unusual even today, but unheard of in the eighties—and he and I became a little team. Mom and Dad made change feel like opportunity, not a threat. When we had to pack up our beautiful house and say goodbye to those brightly colored carpets and the years of family memories in those walls and move into a rented condo across town, Dad made it feel like we were feathering a nest. A *cool* nest, even though it was just a fraction of the size of the house I'd grown up in. Dad put a Ping-Pong table on the uneven concrete basement floor and showed no mercy in our matches. He put an aquarium in the living room and filled it with colorful, tropical fish and—to my delight—a little plastic treasure box. On the main floor, we had a small eat-in kitchen and a little family room with a tube TV where we'd watch recorded VHS tapes of *Saturday Night Live*, laughing our butts off to Jim Belushi, Martin Short, and Eddie Murphy. Upstairs were two small bedrooms and the bathroom we shared. This was a far cry from the pink shag carpeted bedroom in the house we both missed, so to make my room extra special . . . he surprised me with a waterbed. I cannot overstate how cool this bizarre piece of furniture was at the time, and how happy it made me to fall asleep on a big rubber water balloon. Still, when I thought about another little girl walking down the stairs of our old house on Christmas morning or playing in the backyard, I felt myself burn with envy and sadness. To this day, I'll drive by my childhood home any time I'm in Kenosha and get the urge to go weed the garden beds.

The condo was a turnkey property that took some of the pressure off him as a single dad. But I didn't need to know *that*. I just needed to know that whether I was in Kenosha or Chicago, I was loved and cared for. And in Kenosha, Dad was happy to step up to do what my friends' dads wouldn't dream of doing, from stocking my bathroom with tampons to waiting patiently outside of the dressing room in JC Penney. And that, my friends, is a *real* man.

My mother loved me, and she loved her life in Chicago. She had her own apartment in the suburbs, decorated the way she wanted it decorated: a plush, floral couch from Laura Ashley, extra pillows on the bed, not a single piece of sports memorabilia in sight. I slept in the guest room, a perfectly appointed space with a white iron daybed and its own floral theme. She had a tiny Maltese named Angel who was more of a devil, but aside from being nipped at by a yappy little monster, my mother's place was a little nest of femininity in the big city, an oasis of beauty and comfort. As much as I ached for her when I was home in Kenosha, I knew when I visited her why this point in her life was so significant: she was building her own career and her own life. Far away from me, yes, but also (and importantly) on her own. She didn't have a husband paying her bills or giving her advice; she was the captain of her own ship, calling her own shots. I loved watching her get ready for work in the morning. My dad was a stylish man, but all he had to do to get ready for work was to put on a suit and his signature cowboy boots and grab a cup of coffee before he kissed me goodbye. My mother took her time, playing up her innate beauty with her eighties power suits and wide belts, putting all her Mary Kay expertise to work as she "put on a face" every morning. Sometimes, as I fluffed my perm in my mirror before school, I imagined what she was doing in the same moment down in Chicago: What outfit was she wearing today? What shades of eyeshadow would she wear? What would she think of this scrunchie? In my mind, the opening chords to Dolly Parton's "9 to 5" played over a montage of the two of us getting ready: mom in her downtown apartment, me in my bathroom in Kenosha, both of us getting ready to take on our day.

VHS tapes were some of my best friends in those days. Having a VCR was a huge luxury; the first time my dad and I used one, we had rented it from the video store, along with a movie for the two of us to watch for movie night. It was incredible: we could watch a movie without going to a theater, and without any commercial breaks. If the phone rang, we could pause it. If I wanted to hear a joke again, we could rewind. I snuggled up next to my dad, luxuriating in our "home theater" while he read legal briefs and paid just enough attention to laugh at the right times. When my father surprised me by buying our very own VCR, the magic was mine to keep.

My dad's law office was in downtown Kenosha, and his employees were all women with kids at home. They'd greet me warmly when I walked in the door with my heavy backpack and set me up in the conference room or in one of the stately leather chairs in my dad's office. My dad was the boss, and I loved watching him work: how declarative and decisive he was on his phone calls, how confident he was heading into court, and how kind he was to the people he worked with.

"Family first," he'd remind his secretary when she apologized for having to knock off early to pick up her kids. "Get outta here." I swelled with pride at this, and how his employees loved and appreciated him, how loyal they were to their small company. His name was on the door, but the success belonged to everyone. He didn't win cases, he'd remind me, the *team* won cases.

In 2020, women represented only 21% of c-suite executives, meaning that nearly four decades after 9 to 5 came out, there were more CEOs named John than there were female CEOs.

If I didn't walk over to my dad's office after school, I came back to our condo and settled into our couch with some of my favorite ladies: Dolly, Lily, and Jane. *9 to 5* was perhaps not considered a children's movie, but I was essentially a latchkey kid and there were plenty of worse things I could have been doing. Instead, I did my homework while watching three fed-up women take their office (and their jerk boss) into their own hands. Dolly Parton was (and is today) a personal hero of mine: talented, glamorous, and kind. When the world wanted to make her a joke, she beat them to the punchline.

She never apologized for who she was, where she came from, or how she looked, even when she was coloring outside the lines. She had everything a person could want, but she made it a point to share that wealth with other people. This was her first movie role, and if anyone had asked this Midwestern middle schooler for a review, I would have told you it was the best movie ever made. This was the world I longed to inhabit: where women linked arms and moved up the ladder together, where they saw each other not as competition but as comrades, and where yes, the outfits were killer and the theme song impeccable.

At school, this was not my reality. My female peers had apparently never seen this film, or at least not understood the underlying themes of female friendship and empowerment. The waters of middle school turn many girls into sharks, and I was an unsuspecting swimmer looking to tread water until these years were over. I was easy to make fun of: my mom was in Chicago, and I lived alone with my dad. Sometimes, my grandma picked me up from school. My aunt Jo Ann's influence had taught me that with the right clothes, I could become whoever I wanted to be. Her closet mirrors showed me the thrilling power of fashion. This was more than just the right outfit, it was style. But in case you've forgotten your own middle school years, conformity is how you survive. As ready as I was to embrace Dolly's message of being yourself, my individuality made me a target. But I didn't know how to not be myself, so I'd show up to school dressed like an extra from a Madonna video and smile while the other girls threw garbage at me in the hallways. And then I'd head home, pop in a tape, and dream about the future.

The future, by the way, is not here yet. In 2020, women represented only 21% of c-suite executives,[1] meaning that nearly four decades after *9 to 5* came out, there were more CEOs named John than there were female CEOs.[2] The pandemic saw 2.5 million women leave the workforce altogether, crumbling under the pressure of managing the second shift of family life: bearing responsibility for cooking, cleaning, making kids' dental appointments, buying birthday presents.[3] It's obvious that the changes I felt so certain were here when I was a girl are simply not available to the majority of working women. And that, my friends, is bullshit. We all know it! Because just like my mother and plenty of women before and after her, many of us have been forced to choose between work and the rest of our lives.

It's not a false choice. It's one that has real-life consequences. It's a choice that means 2.5 million women sacrificed their ability to build and maintain financial independence, the ability to save for their retirement or pay their own bills. It's a choice that means the workforce is missing out on the skills of 2.5 million women who have something real to offer the world. Years later, my stepfather Rob would look me in the eye and tell me what I already knew: that my mother had been given a choice where nobody won, that the world she lived in was not the world she deserved, that the move hurt her, too. Of course it did! I realize now, she was far from a villain; we were both the heroes and the victims of a story largely written by cultural and structural influences outside of our control. But I wouldn't understand until I was a mother myself.

Before I was a mother, I spent a few years working in ad sales for a travel company. The job was consuming, and I was good at it. It wasn't unusual for me to spend three to five weeks at a time on the road, flying from city to city or island to island, meeting with clients and closing deals. This job looked fun and glamorous on the outside; I got to go island-hopping in the Bahamas . . . for work! But looking at the executives above me, it was clear that there was only so far for me to go in this organization. There was zero female representation in senior leadership, and I was regularly belittled by the same kind of boss that Dolly and her pals had in *9 to 5*. I took what I could from the experience: I paid attention to the way the business ran, and how it was structured. I took advantage of every professional development opportunity they offered. And every time I saw something that made me want to crawl out of my skin, I was learning how *not* to be a boss. When I got a crack at leadership, I wouldn't take credit for people's successes or attack them publicly for their mistakes. I'd make sure that people felt empowered and supported. But in the meantime . . . I was stuck here in the middle of the ladder, wondering how this job could ever work for me when I settled down and had kids. It wouldn't. And when I married my first husband, I left that job knowing that as much as I loved my work, I couldn't have it all. Not yet, at least.

I had strong connections in the Austin business world and a background in branding, marketing, and advertising. Thus, Glitter Public Relations was born. Yes, Glitter. It was 2000, and we were all obsessed with bling, J. Lo, and embellished jeans . . . it was a different time, and let's hope it never returns. I got a few clients and spent a few hours a day working on marketing plans for them: updating their brochures, reaching out to local media, and helping them plan events. But it still didn't scratch the itch that had started when I was a little girl tagging along with Aunt Jo Ann to her fancy fashion job in Milwaukee. I still wanted to work in fashion, but how? I was a stay-at-home mom in Texas, and I couldn't sew to save my life. Doing PR for boutiques was close, but not it, and Glitter was not my destiny. My destiny arrived in the form of two pink lines on a plastic pregnancy test not long after our wedding bells had rung. We were having a baby!

During that pregnancy, I signed up for a jewelry-making class at a local bead shop. I'd made jewelry before, but this was my first formal instruction, sitting around a table with a few other women while the bead shop ladies taught us how to wire wrap, one of the oldest methods of jewelry making. It didn't require soldering or heat, just the careful rhythm of wrapping wire in and around itself and your chosen stones or beads until something beautiful formed in your hands. I loved the feeling of patiently turning a roll of golden wire and a piece of turquoise into a pendant or a pair of earrings, seeing my imagination become material. I left that class with a bag of components: clasps, wire, cord, stones, and beads. I organized them into a small plastic case, a little magic box that held possibility and creativity.

From the moment I saw Cade's beautiful brown eyes, I knew I wanted to be the best mother I could be. But I was also desperate to get back into business . . . this time on my own terms. Cade was born on November 11, 2001, exactly two months after 9/11. The world felt scarier and more uncertain than ever before, but I had my gorgeous baby: full of smiles, committed to a sleep schedule, and happy as a clam whether we were strolling through the park or running errands. I didn't have a job to go back to, but my brain couldn't stop seeing opportunities. Cade and I would step into a coffee shop, and I'd wonder about their financial health and if they'd considered rebranding. And I'd pop into boutiques to try on jewelry and think, this isn't quite what I'm looking for or I can't afford that. I loved natural, semi-precious stones but there was no way I could afford a $200 pair of earrings.

That small plastic case of beads and wire and cord and stones became a bigger plastic case. I filled notebooks with doodles of necklaces and earrings that were far above my skill level, and then spent Cade's epic naptimes hunched over the dining room table trying to make them real. I loved the process, the meditation of manipulating wire into the shapes I saw in my head, combining colors that brought joy to my outfits and my day: coral, turquoise, and citrine.

Now, most of the things I created were not perfect: there was a learning curve, and I was right at the bottom of it for a while. Metal is sharp, and my hands were covered in tiny scabs from poking myself. My cuticles were a mess. But eventually, I got it down. When I could wire wrap with my eyes closed, I learned to silk tie, weaving stones around strips of colorful silk. It felt so good to make something, to take a pile of stone and metal and fabric and turn it into something beautiful. I beamed when women would compliment my jewelry and ask where I'd gotten it.

"Oh," I'd say, not even attempting to suppress my pride. "I made it."

I lived for the gasp that followed, and then the question: "Could you make me one?"

I could make them one, but I'd just as often take it off and hand it to them, then watch joyfully as a fellow mom walked out of Mommy and Me class with a piece of jewelry she loved. My friends and sisters were the first recipients of my excess, but I felt confident enough to take orders from admiring strangers. *They're wearing something I made*, I'd think. *I did that.*

"You really should sell these, Kendra," my best friend, Ashlynn, would say. I'd made her some custom pieces that always got her compliments when she was out and about. I'd thought about it, sure. I'd even asked Cade.

"What do you think, baby?" I'd coo to him. "Can Mommy do this, or is she crazy?" He answered every one of my questions with giggles and smiles that I took as affirmations: go do it, Mom. Be brave. Why was I taking advice from a baby who couldn't even hold up his head on his own? This was a terrible time to start a business! It was impractical in nearly every way. My hobby had quickly turned into a passion, and I saw a market for natural stones and unique designs at a price point that would let women have something beautiful and unique without missing their rent payment. I spent weeks creating a first collection: a cohesive group of french-hook and chandelier earrings and multistrand necklaces where I mixed peridot and light blue topaz, citrine and carnelian, taking stones from nature to create unique color mixes I wasn't seeing anywhere else. Now I just needed a way to present it: there was no money in the budget to buy display forms or boxes, so I looked around my house and took inventory of my options. A shoebox? No.

Tupperware? Noooo. The answer was in the kitchen: a beautiful wooden tea box that John and I had received as a wedding
gift. Could this work? I emptied out the teas and tucked the
earring and jewelry sets into the little dividers. It was perfect,
and it smelled beautiful when I opened it. I imagined myself
swanning in, presenting my collection to slack-jawed salespeo-
ple who would be awestruck by my craftsmanship and
presentation.

I didn't so much swan into these boutiques as stumble.
Cade was strapped into his Baby Bjorn and I had used his
diaper bag as a sort of briefcase, with order forms and
invoices tucked into the front pocket with the butt wipes. I
balanced my purse and the tea box on my right side, and
tried to get through the door as gracefully as possible. I probably looked like a mess, but with a salesman like Cade, coo-
ing and flirting with everyone we met—it worked. Mostly.
The first boutique I walked into turned me away within two
minutes, and I felt my cheeks flush as I walked out. I got
Cade back into the car seat and sat in the front seat trying
not to cry.

"This is so dumb," I said to myself. "Let's just go home
and give away the jewelry." From the backseat, I heard my
sweet little boy giggling. He was still in a great mood, and I
had another hour before it was his naptime. The next boutique on my list was the Garden Room, one of my favorite
places in Austin, and it was just three miles away. I took
Cade's lead and put the car in drive. Patty, the owner, was
working that day and greeted me with the same Texas charm
she'd always shown me. The residual shame from my first
rejection melted away, and while she gushed over Cade, I

mentioned that I now had a jewelry collection, and I'd love to show it to her. She placed an order on the spot, and I pulled the order forms I'd made with WordPerfect out of Cade's diaper bag like I'd done it a million times before. Cade and I went to another shop, where I said confidently, "I'm Kendra Scott, a local jewelry designer, and I'd love to show you my new collection." They placed an order, too. The third shop? Same thing. Right as we were pushing up against naptime, we stopped by our fourth place on the way home, where the owner was prepping for a fashion show and asked to buy the samples. I hadn't planned for this scenario, but I knew I'd spent $500 on the materials and told her she could have them for $1200. She wrote me a check—my very first—on the spot. I walked out with an empty wooden tea box and a check in my hand, literally skipping back to the car while kissing the top of Cade's sweet head.

Your drive and ambition are not measured by the hours you spend with your butt in a seat where I can see you, but by the passion you bring to your job.

"We have a business, baby!" I sang to Cade as I snapped him back into his car seat. While Cade napped, I put the orders up on a little bulletin board in my guest room. I delivered all my orders the next week, wire-wrapping while Cade sat in his bouncy seat or played in his baby gym. A week later, they were calling for reorders. I spent a little bit of money on a babysitter, who I taught to wire-wrap while Cade was napping, and the three of us became a little club in the guest room. I loved being our sales rep. Not everyone was interested in buying jewelry from a woman with a baby strapped to her chest, but the people who were interested placed their orders immediately, and I walked out feeling like a champion. A champion with actual orders to fill.

It didn't take long for the jewelry operation to take over the spare bedroom and then some. My mom and my friends would pack orders in the dining room, I'd make the jewelry in the bedroom, and in between bouts of productivity, we'd play with Cade or listen as he watched *Baby Einstein*. The business was called Kendra Scott Jewelry only because my first business cards—designed in WordPerfect, printed on my ancient home printer, and cut by hand—read:

KENDRA SCOTT
JEWELRY

Creative, right? We didn't have a boss, and I didn't have to choose between my world and my work. The choice my mother was given—her work or her child—would never apply to me, not if I could help it. I could be a wife and a mother and a businesswoman, and nobody was going to stop me. Writing this, I am nobody's wife, and a mother of three beautiful boys. Kendra Scott the company is filled with wives, husbands, mothers, fathers, and partners. We have over three thousand people and hundreds in our headquarters who are working 9 to 5 or 8 to 4 or 7 to 3 or, honestly, I don't really care as long as the work gets done and people feel happy and healthy and fulfilled. Your drive and ambition are not measured by the hours you spend with your butt in a seat where I can see you, but by the passion you bring to your job. And passion and purpose do not exist in a vacuum. They are fueled by the ways we engage with the world. As human beings, our lives are an asset to our careers, not a liability. A person who can draw on their life experiences brings fresh perspective to old problems, they bring compassion and empathy and personality to the workplace, and we need that.

It's on us to make sure that we create environments where the humanity of the people who work with us is not just recognized but respected.

Being passionate about the work means nothing if you aren't passionate about the world, and your place in it. What drives you? Where do you want to be, in or outside of this company? The formula for what it means to be a dedicated and successful person needs to change, and the responsibility for that lies with decision makers in every organization. It's on us to make sure that we create environments where the humanity of the people who work with us is not just recognized but respected. The three central characters of *9 to 5* include a widow and a divorcée, two women whose worlds fell apart and who found themselves as the sole breadwinner for their family. When they put themselves in charge, it was not to pursue power for the sake of power, but to build the kind of workplace that reflected their human needs: they equalized the pay structure, implemented job shares and flexible hours, and set up a daycare program. There is no such thing as leaving life at the door. Our experiences outside of work enrich our lives *at* work. They bring perspective and compassion and empathy and *personality* to the workplace.

My mother modeled for me what a group of supportive, encouraging women could do for and with one another. Mary Kay was more than just a job for her, it was a sisterhood. Their regular meetings in our basement were some of my favorite childhood memories, when the energy in our house transformed and shifted. On these evenings, our street would be lined with station wagons and vans sporting Mary Kay stickers in their back windshields. I would watch as mothers and grandmothers, aunts and sisters would stream up our walkway, through the front door and down into the basement that had been transformed into a Mary Kay paradise. I'm sure I should have been doing homework or going to bed, but I just loved the energy in that room my father had remodeled just for Jan's Jewels and their regular gatherings. These women *were* jewels. They were *fabulous*, a parade of flamingoes in pink jackets, their bedazzled pink pins and brooches adding a sparkle to their look. They were glammed up not for a night on the town, but a night with each other. Starting in a circle, they'd smile and sing their Mary Kay songs:

I've got that Mary Kay enthusiasm down in my heart.
Down in my heart, down in my heart.
I've got that Mary Kay enthusiasm down in my heart.
Down in my heart to stay!

One by one, they'd go around the room and update each other: sales, business challenges, personal lives. They'd pass tissues and cry for each other's struggles, they'd genuinely cheer for each other's wins. These meetings were a chance to learn and grow as professionals and people. They learned the new collections and benefits of new skincare products. They celebrated sales milestones and offered each other genuine advice. They weren't competitors, they were collaborators, and their sincere appreciation of each other felt like watching *9 to 5* in real life. I had my close friend Janet and a few other friends, but what I wanted was this: a place where everyone felt welcomed and celebrated for who they were . . . a sisterhood. My mom's success in Mary Kay wasn't just based on her own sales rankings, but on the success of the women who gathered in that basement "beauty room." These women were genuinely invested in each other personally and professionally, and my little impressionable brain never forgot the feeling of a group of women encouraging and empowering one another, how it's so much easier to believe in yourself when you have other people to believe in you, too.

There is no denying the influence my parents had on who I am personally and professionally, and there's no denying the influence Dolly Parton and *9 to 5* had on me either. Walk through the doors of our headquarters and you'll see a gym that's accessible to every employee, with classes held during the workday so they can prioritize their health and wellness. You can grab a juice from the juice bar or get a complimentary manicure during a meeting with your manager. And when school is unexpectedly canceled or your babysitter bails? Your child is welcome to spend their day with you at your desk or in the playroom we've created just for them. Everyone deserves this, because our life is more than just work. Today alone, while writing this book and running the company, I've stepped out of a board meeting to take a parent-teacher conference and thrown a football with my eight-year-old in between paragraphs. I've ditched out on fancy events to take care of my own father, and I've extended maternity leaves when I can just *tell* someone isn't ready to be back full-time. When your life goes upside down—and it will, without warning—you'll know at Kendra Scott that your company has your back, and I do, too.

As long as my name is on the door and the gift bags and the boxes, nobody will need to choose between their work and their lives.

9 to 5 was a fictional movie, but the reality we've created at Kendra Scott could be replicated by many companies if they stopped to listen to what their employees want and need. It's possible to create a new kind of culture around work that doesn't require employees to kidnap their bosses and hold them hostage in their own homes. No business or

Five

Stickster

"I have confidence, they'll put me to the test . . . but I'll make them see . . . I have confidence in meeeeeee!"

I thought I was singing quietly, but my words echoed through the empty halls and my husband, John, was slightly confused. We were on the way to what I thought might be a life-changing meeting, with a jewelry rep responsible for getting products into the biggest stores in the country, helping me scale beyond local Austin boutiques and onto a national stage.

Just two days before, I'd answered the phone during Cade's naptime to a woman asking, "Is this Kendra Scott?"

"Yes," I'd said, preparing to hang up on a telemarketer.

"Do you make jewelry?" she asked.

"Yes!" I replied excitedly, ready to make a sale.

"Well," she sighed. "I'm a rep here in Dallas and I've got a problem. None of my Austin stores are buying from my lines because they're buying from some local girl named Kendra Scott."

"That's me," I said, not sure if I was in trouble or in luck.

Ten minutes later, I had an appointment to meet her at her showroom in Dallas to show her "my line." I surveyed the guest room, with every surface covered with tools, wire, and jewelry in various states of completion . . . and I got to work. I looked at my printed-at-home business cards and cringed. I typed up a new version and brought it to Kinko's to have it professionally printed with the new professional name that I thought made it sound like a real company: Kendra Scott Jewelry was now Kendra Scott Designs. The tea box had been fine until this moment, but I couldn't walk into a showroom with it. No, I needed a real jewelry case. It hurt to write that check, but I told myself it was an investment in the business. It was, I reminded myself, a business. John was used to meetings like this: he's a skilled negotiator and a respected local businessman, and people like him, so I brought him along to drive the car, to carry the boxes, and to add to the appearance that my business is more than just me, my friends, and sometimes Cade's babysitter making necklaces and earrings in the spare bedroom of our house.

"Is that . . . from *The Sound of Music*?" he laughed, and I nodded, continuing the song and adding in some dance steps. The adrenaline that got me through the past two days had worn off, and from the moment I woke up that morning I'd felt a hot pool of anxiety sitting behind my ribs. What if she hates my designs? What if she thinks I'm too small a brand? What if she turns me down? What am I even doing here? This is not the typical voice that lives in my head, and frankly, I don't like her. I'm naturally a Maria—I see possibility in problems, I'm optimistic to the point of no return, and if I knew how to sew I would love to make matching outfits for myself and my children out of the right set of curtains. *The Sound of Music* might not be the hype song that gets you ready to take on the world, but it works for me, and by the time we reached the elevator, the anxiety had alchemized into excitement.

"You ready, Maria?" John asked with a laugh, and the elevator doors closed, carrying us up to my future.

The last time I'd felt this nervous was probably in the seventh grade. I was known around Kenosha Middle School as Stickster—a hurtful and also extremely accurate nickname that matched my physical description. I was basically a bobblehead: an orange of a head balanced on a tall, lanky toothpick of a body. By middle school, other girls had already gotten boobs and filled out their Esprit leggings. I was . . . well, Stickster. My skinniness wasn't all that was working against me. I was also a little *out there* for small-town Wisconsin.

I took joy in getting dressed for school, even though my closet and my budget were significantly smaller than my Aunt Jo Ann's. I wore Lee press-on nails and splatter paint T-shirts and every loud, wacky thing I could get my hands on, which was hard to do when the hottest shopping spot in town was the outlet mall. If I couldn't find the right piece for my look, I'd try to make it myself: I could cut my T-shirts to look like Jennifer Grey in *Dirty Dancing*, or distress my own jeans. Changing the shoelaces on my Reeboks changed the whole look, and a wristful of jelly bracelets in a rainbow of colors made all the difference. Imagine the outfit you'd wear as a joke to an eighties party: that was probably my favorite outfit in middle school. My dad would patiently sit outside the dressing rooms at the outlet mall while I tried on outfits, and then sit on the couch while I did a one-girl fashion show before school.

"Do you like it?" I'd ask, showing off the neon puffy paint I'd used to decorate my off-brand Keds, or how my scrunchie matched the thread of my sweater, and he'd nod enthusiastically and say, "No. I love it!" I got to start every day with a little shot of confidence before stepping into school and having it all sucked out of me immediately.

Middle school is not considered a pleasant time in adolescence, I know, but my middle school experience seemed particularly miserable. I didn't know that the key to surviving these years is to assimilate, to suppress your individuality and do your best to blend into the herd. Instead, I showed up Monday through Friday ready to be myself: loud, enthusiastic, and dressed like an extra in a music video. This did not make me popular; this made me a target. Girls would switch tables to avoid sitting with me at lunch, leave me off the invite list for birthday parties . . . tear my art down from the hallway bulletin board. And still, I showed up every day willing to try again: I waved hellos that were never returned, I sat down at a cafeteria table and watched as every girl stood up in unison and moved away, I raised my hand when I knew the answer and pretended I couldn't hear everyone behind me giggling. I hummed "I Have Confidence" to myself, having rented it repeatedly from the video store just to write the words down in a notebook to remember for later. And I also spent many lunch periods alone in the girls' bathroom, my feet tucked up onto the toilet seat to avoid getting busted by the hall monitor, who maybe could have been monitoring the kids who were tormenting one another instead of cruising the halls for loners. But this was the eighties, and bullying was considered a non-negotiable part of childhood, a rite of passage. Telling your teachers was unheard of—you'd be a snitch!—sticks and stones could break your bones, but nobody thought that words could break your spirit. The solution was obvious: I needed a makeover.

"I want to look like Sheena Easton," I told my hairstylist. Barb worked out of her house in Kenosha, offering cuts and perms in her kitchen, where I was sitting on a dining chair covered in plastic. I caught a slight look of confusion in Barb's eyes, which I ignored. Sheena Easton was a huge pop star, and her glossy red curls were exactly what I needed to transform myself into the most glamorous middle schooler in Kenosha, Wisconsin. This hairstyle was a Hail Mary, a hope that I could change the narrative around me with a new look. Everyone liked Sheena Easton, so everyone would like me if I looked like her, right? While my hair was being processed, I disappeared into the fantasy of strutting into school on Monday and showing off my new look.

"Who is that?" they'd whisper. "Is that . . . Kendra?"

I was vibrating with excitement and anticipation, the knowledge that I was about to become a whole new Kendra. There was no mirror in the kitchen, so while we listened to Top 40 and chit-chatted about the weather, I trusted Barb to deliver on my vision. My eyes watered with the sour smell of the perm solution, but I told myself it was a small price to pay for jaw-dropping beauty. Once we'd processed, I did a backbend over her linoleum counter so she could rinse me in the kitchen sink. All that was left was the cut, a little shaping to make sure I walked out looking exactly like Sheena. Barb got out the shears and started snipping . . . and man, there was a lot of hair falling to the ground. Like, a lot. But you don't want to doubt an artist, so I just ignored the anxiety boiling up inside of me and told myself it would be worth it. When she handed me the big, pink plastic Goody mirror, I froze my face into what I hoped was a convincing smile. The cascading chestnut curls I was expecting were instead a chestnut explosion of short corkscrew curls springing from my head in every direction. Down my back hung a tightly braided rat tail.

The stylist was excited about her work and handed me a copy of *People* magazine—apparently a more recent issue than the one we had sitting on our coffee table. There, inside of those glossy pages, was a spread about Sheena's new look. She had given me what I didn't know I was asking for, and now I had to go to school like this. I was dead, and I knew it.

My mom saw the truth in my eyes—every woman knows what it's like to lie to save a hairstylist's feelings—and in the car she tried to give me a pep talk.

"It's not so bad" was apparently the best she could come up with, but it was about to get worse. She assured me that in eighteen months it would all be grown out again. Eighteen months? A year and a half? I was in the midst of my first anxiety attack, but I didn't know that. My heart raced, my breath was ragged, and inside of me was a crushing sense of doom. Back at home with my dad, I put on a giant hoodie and pulled the strings tight around my face. I wouldn't even let him see it, because I knew he'd give me the same kind of talk my mom had. After hours of me crying and him pleading with me to just take off the hood, I loosened the ties and lowered it down, the curls springing out around my face.

"It's . . . nice," he said, which is Midwestern for "holy shit." I cried even harder.

"I think you can make anything look good," he said, and he believed that because he'd never been a middle school girl. I locked my bedroom door and cried through the weekend. As a parent, I can't imagine how hard this was for my dad. I was Peak Teenager in this moment, and nothing he could say or do would change how I felt. So, he didn't try to change how I felt. He let me cry, but he didn't let me skip school on Monday. He didn't call the principal and tell him that I needed to be the exception to the "no hats" rule. He didn't play into all of my worst feelings about myself, he just let me have them. And when Monday morning arrived, something was different. I was over the shock of my reflection in the mirror, and I could see that this haircut wasn't what I expected, but it was still, strangely, me. I wasn't like all the other girls in my middle school, and I never would be. More importantly, I didn't want to be. And I didn't want to eat lunch in the bathroom either. Why had I ever done that, anyway? I hadn't done anything wrong! I mean, yes, a rat tail is a violation of fashion, but the punishment of eating a PB&J on the toilet did not fit the crime. Who would benefit from me hiding out and playing dead?

When my dad kissed me goodbye at drop-off, I walked into that middle school with my permed head held high. I sat down at lunch with my friend Janet, and when the meanest girls in our class told me I looked like a mop, I smiled and thanked them and turned back to Janet to continue our conversation. Nobody else had changed their opinion of me, but I had changed my opinion of me. Their behavior didn't change, mine did. Did I still cry after school? Absolutely. But did I hide in the bathroom during lunch? Absolutely not. I was me, take it or leave it (and the overwhelming majority of my classmates did leave it).

I hadn't been Stickster for decades when I walked into that showroom in Dallas, but I wore her same confidence when I sat down across the table from a woman whose power had scared me just a few minutes before. I belong here, I reminded myself, I have confidence in me. I watched as she picked up the pieces I'd been up late at night creating: they're good, I reminded myself, you're good, no matter what she says. And I was right. I hadn't needed new business cards, or a new name, or that jewelry case. I loved John, but I didn't need him to give me any legitimacy (though, yes, I was happy to have had him driving). I knew my stuff, the same way I knew how to trick Cade into eating vegetables or how to layer strands of stones to bring out their colors. I had always been good enough for this meeting, and this buyer knew it. The meeting might have lasted five hours or five minutes, I couldn't have told you. I just knew that on the elevator ride back down to our car, I cried tears of joy: I was in. She was going to represent my line.

That meeting wasn't the hard part of building this business. That was a minor step, a small test of what I would be up against as we moved forward. That showroom meeting and that rep did help bring the business into the next level, and the next level required money. Our first big order was for a department store that wanted 4,500 pieces and wrote a purchase order for $70,000. It was a staggering amount of money—more than I'd ever seen at one time in my life—and I had no idea how I would fill the order as I signed it. I needed materials—a lot of them. And people—good ones. And I needed more money up front to cover the costs. I walked into my local bank with that purchase order and asked for a line of credit worth $70,000. But I still needed my father-in-law, an attorney who had banked there for decades, to convince them to give me a chance. That worked for a while, but not forever, and you can only go so far with lines of credit and cash-back credit cards and the free version of QuickBooks.

⌒

The right kind of investor can be rocket fuel for a brand, and I would eventually need it. As I'm writing this, access to capital is still notoriously harder for women and people of color to acquire, and it certainly wasn't easy when I started courting investors. Kendra Scott Designs gained steam during the dot-com boom, when investors were all clamoring to invest in websites and vague ideas, not tangible retail products created by hand by a mother in Texas. I'd walk into big, cold conference rooms filled with men in gray suits, and open up a PowerPoint deck bursting with color. I'd pass around the jewelry I made and tell the story I'm telling you: how I loved fashion and jewelry, how I wanted something substantial but not expensive, something stylish but not disposable, how I'd found the white space in the market and intended to fill it. And I'd watch as their eyes glazed over, how they ignored the numbers and the opportunity and instead asked me to be something I wasn't: a tech startup, a useless website that would crash and burn into obscurity, a man in a gray suit. My dad had warned me about Men in Suits. He had been a small-town lawyer stepping into the courtroom to argue against big-city, big-budget firms representing some of the biggest businesses in the Midwest. "Kendra," he told me when I started to court investors, "you're going to be in a lot of meetings with a lot of men in suits. Don't you ever let a man in a suit intimidate you." Every room we step into, whether we're invited or we push our way in, we're stepping into a perception that people have of us: of our capabilities, our value, our worth. It's the easiest thing in the world to believe what people say about you, to let their opinion of you be the deciding factor in whether or not you move forward. For years, I left those meetings without an investment, but with my head held high, knowing that I wasn't wrong about my vision or my business.

Meanwhile, Kendra Scott Designs was bursting out of the spare bedroom and we needed an actual office. I'd scour the *Austin American-Statesman* for office spaces to rent and found an amazing space that was inside a beautiful Victorian house that had been converted into offices many years ago on the hip street of West Sixth. I went to tour the office space and loved the owner, Mike, who owned a sandwich shop company and was also from Wisconsin originally. The office he showed me had big, old windows, high ceilings . . . and a price tag I couldn't afford. I thanked him for his time and got ready to leave when he mentioned that they had an attic office available if I was interested. We walked up a creaky set of steps to the smallest, dingiest space I'd ever seen. Thick green shag carpeting lined the floors, and it smelled like . . . thick, old green shag carpeting. But natural light streamed through the dormer windows, and something about it felt . . . perfect. I signed a lease on the spot and came back that weekend to shampoo the carpet, scour the bathroom, and move in a mini-fridge my mom wasn't using anymore. The lease came with a handful of parking spaces, so it was a race to see who got a spot and who had to circle the neighborhood looking for parking. We tucked our desks and worktables into the dormer windows, passing back and forth the one set of tools we had to work with because every penny that came in and out mattered and everyone in the office knew it. Cade's pack and play sat in the middle of the room, and we'd all take turns playing with him or feeding him or reading him stories. I will always be thankful for Mike, who would take my rent check every month and ask, "Is this okay to cash today?" Sometimes it wasn't—we were selling to a large department store and smaller retailers who paid their invoices on a net 60 or net 90 timeline, and balancing the books felt like a shell game some months. I probably called the bank at least twice a day to confirm we hadn't overdrawn. But Mike never held it against me, just held on to the check until I came downstairs to give him the all clear. We weren't growing at a speed that would interest investors, but we showed up every day to that

Six

Detour to Destiny

May 18, 2018
Graduation Day
McCombs School of Business, University of Texas

No other generation in human history is likely to see a level of transformation as profound as the changes you will experience—and even lead—in technology, science, business, government, and life. You have been taught by the best. But we, your elders—much as I hate to use that term—have not seen what you will see. We've watched life-changing technologies come and go. I remember my family's first VCR and answering machine. Those were once groundbreaking products! My point is your teachers, your parents, all of us—all we can do is give you the playbook. But you have to adapt it to a rapidly changing game.

You must learn to pivot quickly and adjust to what's happening around you, and to sometimes let go of your ideas of how things should be or what you want.

—KENDRA SCOTT

A commencement speech is a big responsibility for a speaker: you're one of the last voices a student will hear before they cross the stage and become a graduate. I practiced my speech for hours—standing in front of the mirror, running on a treadmill, to the boys over dinner—and still my hands shook when I first stepped up to the podium. I wanted to knock it out of the park for these kids and for the parents who had invested so much of their time and love and energy into getting to this moment. My mother sat in the front, watching proudly as her daughter gave an inspiring speech to kids who could very well end up applying to her billion-dollar company. But that's just the highlight reel, and it was important to me that these kids know that as perfect and shiny as some things look, they don't always work out the way you'd planned.

I'd always imagined that I'd leave Wisconsin someday, but I hadn't thought about what that would look like, and it all felt so far away. Middle school ended, and high school began, and even though things were a little better socially, it was still only a little better. I was a square peg in a round town, trying my best to care about writing papers and studying for midterms but much more interested in making sure I got whatever fashion magazines were available at the drugstore the minute they were unboxed. The kids who were into academics at my high school were ridiculed and mocked for being nerds. Doing well academically was a punishable offense socially, where the "cool" kids were focused on partying. This was not an environment where I could succeed, and I missed forty-seven days of school my sophomore year, leaving during lunch to spend the rest of the day sitting on the rocks at Lake Michigan, dreaming of a life I wished I had. I hated that school, and looking back knowing what I know now about mental health, I'm sure that I was clinically depressed. I knew there was something else out there for me, but I didn't know how to get it.

Meanwhile, my mother had married a man named Rob and moved from Chicago all the way to Houston, Texas, a city so far away from me that it might as well be Paris or Milan. My travels so far had been limited to the upper Midwest, and mostly road trips, so when my mom offered to fly me down to visit her and her husband over the summer, I said yes before the question was even fully out of her mouth. I hadn't ever been away from my dad for more than a few nights other than sleepovers with friends or a visit to Mom's place in Chicago, but a summer spent away from Kenosha felt like an opportunity I couldn't pass up.

"I'll be fine, Kendra," Dad reassured me when we hugged goodbye at the gate. "I know how to take care of myself." He did, I knew, but I still cried in his arms until the flight attendants insisted that I board the plane. I was still crying when the plane lifted off and Wisconsin disappeared into a blur of green miles beneath me.

I stepped off the plane right into the heat of a Houston summer and into my mother's arms. Texas truly felt like another world. The city seemed to sprawl out forever in every direction, and palm trees lined the streets of Mom and Rob's neighborhood, swaying in the wind like they were personally waving hello to me. Their house was a redbrick two-story with big pillars in front and a lush garden that made it feel like a tropical paradise . . . and a kidney-shaped pool in the backyard. Had I accidentally landed in Hollywood? The house looked like it belonged in a soap opera (this is a compliment): picture white carpeting, floral pastel sofas, and lots of dried or fake flowers displayed in big vases. My room had a jack-and-jill bathroom connecting to my sister Diana's room, with a white iron daybed and a matching desk. Every day, I watered what seemed like a hundred potted plants that my mother had surrounding the house, and then I wandered around with the endless number of neighborhood kids my age, kids who were nice and fun, who thought my accent was funny and had lots of questions about Wisconsin and cows.

At night, Rob would come home from work, and he and I would watch hours of TV, talking and laughing and getting to know each other. I'd met him before, but that's much different from living with a person. Everything I knew about stepdads was from TV or movies, which made stepparents out to be evil at best, especially when it came to having a teenage stepkid in the house. And what I knew about Rob was that he had two sons from a previous marriage and a purple heart from serving two tours in Vietnam, that he liked things neat and tidy and he spoke five languages. What was he going to do with a teenage girl from Wisconsin who loved fashion? Well, he was going to win her over without even trying. Rob was so warm and kind and electric, with a deep, olive tan and a megawatt smile and a big, booming laugh. From the moment I got to the house, he made sure I felt like it was our house, that I belonged. On weekends, we'd both lay out by the pool trying to compete for who could get the deepest tan (forgive me, dermatologists, we didn't know better!) and he'd make me a virgin margarita to sip on. And then . . . he'd listen. He'd listen to me talk about high school and why I hated it, about the boy up the street who asked me on a date, about a pair of shoes I wanted to buy. I knew I could tell him anything and he'd hold it in confidence. The weeks flew by, and suddenly it was time to leave. This time, it was my mom and Rob walking me to the gate and drying my tears as we said goodbye.

———

Wisconsin was the same as it ever was, but after those weeks in Houston, it felt even smaller. I missed the warmth, not just the weather and the sunshine, but how friendly and open everyone was to me that summer. I missed the neighborhood kids who had become my friends, and my virgin margaritas by the pool with Rob. Physically, I was getting ready to go back to school, but mentally I was planning my next trip to Houston. And then the phone rang.

My mother was a wreck, but through her sobs she told me that Rob had been in an accident: he'd been driving and had a seizure behind the wheel. His car had smashed into a neighbor's house, and luckily nobody had been seriously injured. But there was more: a brain scan had shown that Rob had an aggressive brain cancer, and nobody knew how long he had to live. There are moments in life where time slows down, and then stops entirely. This was one of them: the clock on the kitchen wall had stopped ticking, the world itself had stopped spinning, and all I could hear was the voice in my head telling me what I had to do next. I needed to leave Kenosha and go back to Houston as soon as possible. Life was shorter than I thought, and Rob's could be ending. I told my dad when he got home from work, and I watched his heart break as he took in the words. I had never broken anyone's heart before, and I'd never wanted to hurt my father. It felt like I was betraying him and all that he'd done for me over the past six years. It felt like I was abandoning him here in the little nest he'd built for us. It felt like I was letting him down. Was I *sure*? he cried. *Was I sure?*

I was. We went to bed that night with tear-soaked faces, each of us crying for different reasons. Dad didn't want me to go, and I knew that I couldn't stay. I knew—as much as you can know anything when you're sixteen—that I had to leave. That I had to shatter my father's world in order to create the one I needed to survive. That if I didn't take this moment, I would regret it forever. My father, I knew, would forgive me. My mother and Rob, I knew, needed me. But more importantly, *I* needed me. I needed *this*. I needed to go.

Two weeks later, I was enrolled in Klein High School—go Bearcats!—and back in that room with the white carpeting and the white iron daybed, spending time after school visiting with Rob. At Mom and Rob's house, I wasn't always an only child. Rob's sons—ten and six years old—were often around, and I went from the baby of the family to an older sister. I learned from the best, big-sister wise, and I loved giving them advice or helping them with homework, and letting them cry in my room about Rob. Because Rob was *their* dad, *their* rock, and they'd already lost their biological mother to ovarian cancer just a few years before. Rob's beautiful brown hair—perfectly graying at the temples—had been shaved for the surgery, which left a winding scar around his scalp like the stitching on a baseball. The chemo and radiation made him sleepy, but he greeted me after school with his bright smile and we'd lay out by the pool to make sure he maintained his golden tan. Rob never tried to be my dad, but he became a father figure to me, and my own father was strong enough to let another man help raise his daughter. As far as stepdads go, Rob was the best one I could possibly imagine. Right when I moved to Texas, he brought me on a tour of Dell Computers, where he worked. He had a family photo of all of us in a frame on his desk, and he introduced me to everyone in the office as his daughter. He'd only been a father to two boys, but he didn't miss a beat. You know how some men joke around about wanting to make sure their daughters' dates know who's the boss? Well, I found out after one of my first dates in Houston that while I was upstairs putting on fake eyelashes and lip gloss, my date was watching my stepdad clean his guns while getting a lecture about my curfew and what it means to respect a woman. That boy respected me so much he wouldn't even hold my hand . . . and I didn't get a second date. Rob always laughed his ass off at that story. I feel lucky that I didn't have to feel caught between Rob and my dad, and lucky to have both of them as confidants and cheerleaders, offering me unconditional love and telling me that they were proud to have a daughter like me. Both of them encouraged me to

For a lot of people, college feels mandatory: it's something our parents expected of us, especially if they didn't get the opportunity to go themselves. For generations, we've been told that it's the path to success, that without it, we'll end up going nowhere fast. I knew that my dad's parents had saved their entire lives to make sure he could go to college and law school, and that my dad expected me to finish school with a degree. I also wasn't used to keeping secrets from my dad: for six years, he'd been my primary parent and my best friend. He was the first person I told when I got my period, and he was the person I cried to when I was being bullied. Every day that I didn't tell him how I felt about school felt like a lie I couldn't escape from, and on Christmas break back in Wisconsin, I finally broke. We were sitting at the dining room table in our little house, eating dinner together like we had every night for six years. But every bite felt like it was stuck in my throat, and finally I broke.

I cried into my mashed potatoes about how much I hated college. I told my dad—who was a bit dumbstruck at this emotional outburst—that I knew what I was supposed to do with my life, and that it wasn't sitting in a classroom all day. I didn't have the grades to get into a business school, so the classes that interested me weren't available to me. I kept going, crying about seeing Rob's head red and irritated from rubbing against his baseball hats, about how much I loved fashion and about how I thought I could have a business selling hats and that some of the profits could go to cancer research and that this was what I was supposed to do and I don't think I took a breath until months of thoughts and feelings were sitting on the table between the two of us. My face was red and wet from all the crying, and when I looked into my dad's eyes, all I saw was pure love. He reached out to wipe the tears from my cheeks and smiled.

"Okay, Kendra," he said. "Let's do hats."

It was that simple to him: I knew who I wanted to be, and he wasn't going to tell me any differently. His own path had diverged widely from his parents', and he wasn't here to get me to follow in his footsteps but to help me find my own footing. The rest of the dinner, we talked through what I knew needed to be done: Where would I get the inventory? Where would I put the store? How would I tell people about it? I loved hearing my dad's perspective, from his years of running his own law office, and he was impressed by how much I'd already soaked up from two semesters in college. I went to bed that night feeling better than I had in months, and when I woke up to leave for the airport, my father surprised me the way his own father had thirty-some years before.

"Kendra," he said, "I've been saving to send you to college since you were born, and if you're done with college, then there's no better use for this money than to be your first investor." The check he handed me made my jaw drop: I had $20,000. I tucked the check into my wallet, where I checked about ten times a day to make sure it was still there. This was more money than I'd ever seen in my entire life—certainly more than I'd ever imagined having at this age—and it was mine. It wasn't just the money, it was what it represented: this was money my dad had worked for on those long nights next to me on the couch, or while I was sitting in his conference room doing my homework. It was the literal fruits of his labor, and he'd used it to invest in me like his own father had invested in him. I still get chills about it to this day. I couldn't have spelled the word "entrepreneur" without consulting a dictionary, but that's exactly what I was. Dropping out of college wasn't a detour, it was setting me on a path toward my destiny.

It's not that college wasn't for me, or that I don't believe in higher education. But my interest in fashion and design had labeled me as a left-brained "creative," and my so-so grades had slammed the doors to any business programs. The gates were closed to anyone who didn't fit the bill for what an entrepreneur "should" look like, and as soon as I got the power to open them, that's what I did. In 2019, I founded the Women's Entrepreneurial and Leadership Institute at the University of Texas at Austin. It's a program that's open to any student in any major, regardless of their background: teachers, engineers, art majors. Anyone who feels a tug toward entrepreneurialism and leadership can enroll in our cross-disciplinary courses and learn how to apply the entrepreneurial mindset to their lives and careers. The point is not fitting into a mold but creating your own and bridging any gaps between left- and right-brained thinking. I'm biased, but I think that creatives actually make the best entrepreneurs, so I made sure to set that institute up in the last place many people would expect to see it: the fine arts building. In the years since, when I'm asked for business advice, I always say to do your own thing, that the minute you find yourself doing what everyone else is doing . . . you've already lost. So I took that check from my dad and set out to do whatever nobody else was doing . . . hats.

Seven

You Do Good

*B*ack in Austin, I learned that $20,000 was not quite the windfall I thought it was, even by 1995 standards. I called local wholesalers to price out inventory, drove around the city looking for storefronts to rent, and trolled the auction notices in the local paper to buy our displays from businesses that were closing. My mom and I built out every inch of that store ourselves, and even then, my bank account was dwindling to nearly empty before I even opened the doors of the Hat Box.

I realized very quickly the first lesson of entrepreneurship: you can't be in it for the money. There was no money to pay myself once I'd signed the lease in the worst corner of the worst mall in town. "Let me help," my mom said. She'd already been side by side with me, installing Home Depot shelf brackets and plywood shelving, but she wrote me a check to help me get the doors open. We'd spent weeks painting and building out the store with materials I'd scavenged from liquidation sales, tracking my inventory in a notebook and tagging every single hat by hand. I went to bed at night with my entire body aching, but with a smile on my face.

Rob's cancer was getting worse, no matter how much he tried to hide it. Astrocytoma is an incurable form of brain cancer, and even with aggressive treatment at one of the best hospitals in the world, the cancer kept progressing. Rob wasn't just a handsome man and the life of the party, he was *smart*. From his time in the service, he spoke five languages fluently. When he started losing words, or tripping over his sentences, he'd try to play it off with a joke or tell us "never mind," like it wasn't important. But it was important: he was losing parts of himself, and there was nothing we could do to stop it. Rob always had a powerful presence, and so we noticed when he started to miss a step or when he'd drop something accidentally. The little things became bigger, and soon he was struggling to form sentences or walk without help. The man who could talk my ear off all night would struggle to say just a few words. But every time we left each other, he'd squeeze my hand and say "love you."

I channeled all of my fear and grief into the Hat Box, and I expected big things for myself: a line out the door on opening day, a hundred stores opening across the country, everyone in the nation returning to the golden age of fashion where your outfit simply wasn't complete without a hat and me funding the brain cancer research that would save my stepdad's life. What can I say? Dream big or not at all.

My first day, the only people who came were Rob and my mother. Leaving the house meant he needed a wheelchair, so a trip to the mall for the two of them was no small task. I was thrilled to see his million-dollar smile while my mom pushed him across the threshold, and then embarrassed: there was literally nobody here, and this store had been inspired by him. But Rob wasn't embarrassed. I watched his eyes move across the space my mother and I had built, and his mouth started to move. I could tell how frustrating it was for him to not be able to express his thoughts. He had a brilliant mind and a quick wit, but the words got stuck between his brain and his tongue. He squeezed my hand while he tried to form the words. I kneeled down in front of him to look him in the eye.

I was doing good, I would do good. This— these words—were my life's purpose.

"It's okay," I said. "I know you're proud of me." He squeezed my hands harder and shook his head no. He *wanted* to speak. Tears formed in his eyes, and then in mine. Listening to Rob had been one of my favorite things. Even when I was a boy-crazy teenager, he'd never lectured me. He'd reminded me that I had gifts and purpose bigger than any ol' boy, and that it was my duty to use and protect the gifts I'd been given. He'd slip these pearls of wisdom in during commercial breaks while we watched *Walker, Texas Ranger* or while we laid out in the backyard, and I'd smile and get back to the story about my newest crush. But today, I would hang on whatever words Rob could get out. I would remember them for the rest of my life. The words came, slowly and methodically, and I do remember them.

"You. Do. Good."

You. Do. Good. I'm sure there was more he *wanted* to say, more wit and wisdom to fill in the cracks, but this was all I needed. I knew exactly what Rob meant, what those words meant to me, what they *would* mean to me. I was doing good, I would do good. This—these words—were my life's purpose. My mom brought him home that day with an angora Kangol's driver hat, and I waited all day for another customer. There wasn't one.

I waited and waited, and not a single other soul passed through those doors. I called my dad sobbing, apologizing for wasting his money.

"It'll get better, honey," he reassured me. "This is part of the process."

It did not get better. When customers did come in, they seemed confused. All I sold were . . . fashion hats? Not winter hats? Not baseball hats? I thought on my feet and told them I could order whatever kind of hat they wanted, and soon I had jester hats, fishing hats, berets, church hats, derby hats . . . and still hardly any sales. If you needed something to go on your head, I'd find it for you. I'd envisioned a bustling store with regular customers, but on my very busiest day—ten hours straight standing at the mall—I had three customers. I mean, three *paying* customers. At least once a week I'd be chasing a shoplifter through the mall, leaving my store (and the cash box) completely unattended. The mall was not a good location, and I'd signed a yearlong lease to get the monthly rent down, so I was trapped. Luckily, I knew a good attorney. It didn't feel great to call my dad and tell him that I'd signed a bad deal, but he stepped in and negotiated my way out, and I found a better location in a better mall, with a month-to-month lease. I still didn't have the money to pay myself, but I took everything I learned from that first build-out and applied it to this store: I faux-finished the walls to look "Texas-Tuscan Chic" and made a sign from giant foam letters I'd spray-painted to look like metal. My location still wasn't great, but the mall had much more traffic and even though I was on the top floor, I was next to a Dillard's department store, which meant much more foot traffic. I finally had enough money to hire a part-time person, a woman in her fifties with a popular newsletter who was known as the Hat Lady of Austin. When I say newsletter, I mean a physical, printed newsletter that was mailed to her subscribers, and having her even part-time meant more customers . . . and a little bit of time off my feet.

By now, the initial investment from my dad was gone, and Rob's brain cancer was only getting more aggressive. Brain cancer is insidious: a cluster of cells reproducing and expanding in the center of your mind, growing like tentacles and destroying the essence of who a person is. The treatments have barely advanced in the past thirty years, and they're invasive (brain surgery) and brutal (chemotherapy and radiation). The big, booming Rob that I'd gotten to know over the summer before junior year of high school, who loved listening to girl talk and tanning in the backyard with me, was small and gray, even with his tan. He'd spent six years embracing every day even with this incurable illness: always ready with his movie-star smile and a listening ear, the sun in our universe. Every time I visited, I'd bring him a new hat, and he'd model it for me. When he could speak, it was always those same three words: You. Do. Good. I was trying, but the Hat Box was failing, and it wasn't *just* a business but a purpose directly tied to my love for Rob. We'd been able to write a few small checks toward cancer research, but it didn't seem like enough when Rob was disintegrating in front of us.

The problems my business was facing could be solved today with some targeted social media ads, but that wasn't an option in the pre-Google era. I had to find a way to connect with people in real life, where they were. And thus, the Hat Racks were born. Well, hat racks had existed for ages, but I spun off pop-up consignment racks in country clubs, gyms, and other small retail shops where I could curate selections of hats for their target market: wide-brimmed visors for the golfers, stylish fashion hats for boutiques, baseball caps and beanies for the gym rats. I scoured secondhand stores and garage sales for vintage hat racks and stocked them at the beginning of every month with inventory targeted to their clientele and stopped in at the end of the month to check the inventory and write invoices. The hosting store or business would take a cut of the profits, and I was finally relieving some of the pressure. The Hat Racks covered the rent on the store and also helped me build relationships with retailers like Patty at the Garden Room, the first boutique to buy my jewelry years later.

Rob was on hospice care now, and the hospice center had delivered a hospital bed to Mom and Rob's beautiful home.

They'd tried to set it up in the spare bedroom, but Rob stopped them. He didn't want to be stuck in the back room, he wanted to be in the living room, in the center of the action, surrounded by the people who loved him. Plus, we joked, we could open the blinds on the picture window to keep his tan. Turns out, that wasn't much of a joke and he actually did ask us to do that, closing his eyes in peaceful gratitude as he felt the warmth of the Texas sun on his skin. Rob was dying, and the unfairness of it all was enough to make me scream on my car rides home. He was only forty-seven years old. He and my mother would never get to retire and travel the world together, to visit the places where Rob spoke the languages fluently from his years as an army brat. He wouldn't get to know my future children, or his sons'. My mother would become a widow. And still, Rob smiled his million-dollar smile. He couldn't speak, but he had spent years telling us how happy he was, how proud of us, how much he loved this family. This family was one he had never expected, and I hadn't either. I hadn't foreseen a stepdad who felt like a second father, or two little brothers. I hadn't imagined that a "broken" family could feel this whole, this complete. We spent every moment of hospice care taking turns so that he'd never be alone. On October 1, 1998, after a late-night shift with Rob, I woke up in my mom's bed to my sister Diana whispering to me that it was time. I knew exactly what she meant, and a sick, sad feeling settled into my chest. In the living room, our mother was weeping next to the love of her life. When he took his last breath, I felt myself lose my own. But my pain was nothing compared to our mother's. She clung to Rob's body, screaming and crying in a voice I hope meal that we exchanged numbers. Weeks later, after sudden and dramatic roommate changes (who doesn't have these in their twenties?), we ended up sharing a tiny one-bedroom apartment and our lives. I was stressed about the Hat Box, I was grieving Rob, I had just been dumped, and I woke up every morning to a fresh daisy in a little vase by the side of my bed. We only had one closet, so I kept my clothes stacked on top of our washing machine. Ashlynn was my instant soul mate, and soon we were moving into a little house on Nasco Drive in the Allandale neighborhood of Austin. It was a life-size dollhouse for two girls in their twenties, complete with a clawfoot bathtub in a nice 1980s mauve. Within days of moving in, we'd painted every single wall, rearranged our furniture about a dozen times, and thrown a raging party. Any minute that we weren't working, Ashlynn and I were together. Half the time we got dressed to go out, we'd meet up in the living room and find we were wearing the exact same thing. So it made perfect sense when Ashlynn wanted to set me up with her boyfriend's best friend.

His name was John Scott, and he was a handsome local entrepreneur who looked like John F. Kennedy Jr. and whose energy and enthusiasm matched my own. John had his own businesses to run, but his were working and mine was working me into the ground. I'd miss dates because I was too exhausted to go out, totally oblivious that I was standing up my future husband and the father of my first two boys. After years of only paying myself sporadically, I got a day job working in ad sales so I could afford to pay someone to look after the store. I'd spend the entire day busting my ass at work, and then rush to the store to do inventory and balance the books.

I'd show up at work exhausted and practically sleep through dinner dates with John. I was cracking apart, but how could I stop? My dad had believed in me, Rob had believed in me, I had believed in me. My Hail Mary idea to save the business was . . . a location next to a grocery store? Brilliant, Kendra. The dream I'd had was a nightmare: Rob had died, and now my business was on its last legs.

It was John who said what I'd been thinking and was too afraid to say.

"Kendra," he said, "what would happen if you let it go?" I let myself imagine the feeling of having only one job that actually paid me, of not having to chase invoices and cross my fingers hoping the checks I wrote to cover my own supplier invoices would actually clear. It felt . . . like freedom. It felt like peace. Rob hadn't said "You work yourself to the bone and ruin your life." He'd told me: you do good. I had done good. And there was more good I could do. Not by bashing my head against a wall trying to make hats a thing but by moving on. John was right: it was time.

Closing a business is even harder than opening one. There's no dream on the horizon to run toward, just a finish line where the ribbon has already been cut and the crowds have gone home, like coming in dead last in a race against yourself. Piece by piece, I dismantled everything I built. I notified the landlord that I'd be vacating my space and let the vendors know that I'd be liquidating. I put up notices in the window and watched as everything I'd built sold for pennies on the dollar. But that sick, sad feeling went away when I saw that the people buying my displays were just like I had been back when I started: working toward their own dreams and goals, hoping that their own Big Idea would hit. I hoped that the things I'd built with my mom and dad would bring them luck, that they were infused with the same energy we'd put into building them. I went to work every day a little less tired, and felt some life returning to me.

On the last day of my lease, I drove to the Hat Box for the very last time. I swept and vacuumed, removing every trace of myself and this dream. I hadn't accounted for the many crying breaks I would take on the floor, so by the time I was finally finished, it was nearly dinnertime. The empty parking lot had filled up with people grabbing groceries for dinner, whose worlds were trucking along as expected while I was having a pivotal life experience! I was acutely aware that these were my last moments with the store: the last time I'd wipe the window, the last time I'd take out the trash. And now, the last time I'd turn the sign in the window, from *Yes, We're Open!* to *Sorry, We're Closed!*

I locked the door for the very last time, openly sobbing among people streaming into the grocery store, and felt a big, fat Texas raindrop hit the top of my head. More followed, and I was in a sudden downpour, watching people sprint with their grocery carts to their station wagons, heading for cover. I, however, was laughing. I'd been looking for signs of Rob everywhere—in cardinals on the bird feeder, lucky pennies on the sidewalk—and here was one. If I wanted to be dramatic, Rob would turn the drama up a notch. The downpour was sudden and short, and in a few minutes the entire parking lot looked like it had been washed clean.

He always did have a great sense of humor and a flair for the dramatic. I was laughing through my tears, and when I turned for one last glance at the store, I saw it. A sign. A *real* sign. That sign I'd flipped before I left. Either I'd done it wrong or it had a mind of its own because from where I stood on the curb, it read: *Yes, We're Open!*

Was I open? I'd been so focused on the closing of the Hat Box and the finality of every action. What if I were *open*? What if I stopped telling myself that I was done with entrepreneurship, that my dream had died. What if I started telling myself that I was open to the possibilities to come. I'd let myself feel all the worst feelings and the worst thoughts: that I was a failure, and that I had not done good. But the Hat Box was my college degree and my MBA rolled into one. I wasn't leaving with nothing. I was leaving with the kind of education I couldn't have gotten from any book. The greatest thing I'd learned was to dare to think differently.

Sometimes, a sign is literally just a sign.
But sometimes it's more.

Sometimes, a sign is literally just a sign. But sometimes it's more. Sometimes it's your future best friend writing her name on a paper tablecloth, or a trip that changes the course of your life. Sometimes it's a reminder from the universe to stop obsessing over what was and open yourself to what could be. I noticed that the dark clouds were gone entirely, and the world was bathed in the soft golden light of a Texas sunset. I didn't bother flipping the sign. I left it there for whoever else may need the same message. I'd need that message plenty of times myself in the years to come: every time the universe shook my personal snow globe without permission. Through nightmare jobs and devastating loss, I've had to remind myself a thousand times that the end of one thing is the beginning of another, even if it isn't a beginning I chose.

And if I could go back in time and ride shotgun with that sad woman weeping in her car while she drove away from the store she thought was going to be the Next Big Thing, I'd tell her that doing good doesn't always mean you win, that you can be proud of yourself for what you've done without shaming yourself for what you haven't. And most importantly, I'd tell her that the next time she opened a business, she'd turn it into a billion-dollar brand.

Behind Every Strong Woman

All women are expected to be superheroes: to do it all, look good doing it, and assure you *it was no problem, really!* I hate this lie; I hate what it does to us, and how it tears us apart from each other by creating and perpetuating a false standard that literally none of us can live up to. Any woman who says she has found the secret to perfect balance is either lying or concealing the truth. Add to that the mythology of entrepreneurs, who are always talked about as though they're lone wolves and singular visionaries who operate outside of the norm. We hold them up on pedestals and admire them for their individualism and their non-conformity. And yes, there are certain characteristics that the entrepreneurs I know tend to have in common: a tolerance for risk, an ability to adapt to change more quickly than others, and a certain brand of confidence and decisiveness that makes people want to jump on board a train that's running full speed on tracks that are still being built. But there is no entrepreneur who has done it all on their own, especially not me. Today, the team at Kendra Scott is around three thousand. But in those early days, there were just a handful of us. We didn't just work together, we rocked each other's babies and dried each other's tears, talked through budgets and made decisions on where we were going together.

It was 2005, in that little attic office. We were still making samples with one set of shared tools between us, trays of stones and spools of wires spread across a shared workspace where Leah and Denise would pass the tools back and forth making samples. Cheryl, who did our graphic design and branding, had a makeshift photo studio with pieces of posterboard propped up on a table in the corner. I ran sales and marketing and jewelry design and anything else that needed doing from my little desk.

Any woman who says she has found the secret to perfect balance is either lying or concealing the truth.

I was never just hiring for a skillset, but to create a team. It didn't matter if you had years and years of experience or a gold-plated resume; if you were a bitch or a mean girl, you weren't going to get a job with us. We were a team like my mom's Mary Kay group, Jan's Jewels, even though Leah would rather die than wear something pink and sparkly and we didn't

BEHIND EVERY STRONG WOMAN

sing songs before our workday. Interviews were and still are about more than just reviewing a resume or asking someone about their strengths and weaknesses: I want to know what a person cares about, what lights them up inside, what's important to them, what they value. Because work can be fun, but it's also work, and you need to be surrounded by people who share your passion even when it means sharing a room in a rat-infested Midtown Manhattan hotel for a trade show.

Every year, tens of thousands of people crowd into the Meat-packing District of New York City for the Accessories Circuit Trade Show: buyers looking for new brands to carry in their stores, suppliers looking to ink new deals, and designers like us hoping to secure some new sales contracts. Our rep had told me that she was happy to go to these trade shows to sell on our behalf, but I knew from going to these trade shows with my rep that there was nobody who could sell Kendra Scott like, well, Kendra Scott. So in 2005, Denise, Cheryl, and I packed our bags and flew economy class to New York City to do the trade show all on our own. We were giggling with excitement the entire ride: can you believe we're doing this? It felt like a vacation with girlfriends, even though we knew we'd been putting in long days at the trade show trying to close some sales. Our displays and samples had all been shipped ahead of time, so all we had to do was go set up and we were free until the next morning, when the doors would open and buyers would certainly flock to us and buy everything we'd designed.

We stepped into the building and were instantly overwhelmed by the scene. We'd rented a "booth" that was approximately ten feet wide, and we'd made a plan for how to make it cute on a budget. Each booth came with a plain white pop-up wall with built-in shelving, and we had packed wallpaper to give it a little life. The jewelry, we figured, would take center stage. How cute. Because every other brand there had set-ups that we hadn't even imagined; their booths were more like small stages, with walls and furniture, interactive digital displays . . . I'm pretty sure there was more than one smoke machine. Cheryl caught my eye, and for a brief second I could tell what we were both thinking: *oh shit.* We needed a map to find our booth, another map to figure out where our boxes were, and approximately eight hours to unpack and set up everything. We quickly realized, making small talk with the people next to us, that the people setting up these very professional-looking booths were people who professionally designed and built out trade show booths for brands. We felt like the only brand setting up its own booth, and even though we'd brought click and snap wood flooring and IKEA furniture and made cute signs and brochures and displays . . . we looked like a dollar store on Fifth Avenue. These other brands had spent literally tens or even hundreds of thousands of dollars on their booths; that was the amount of money we were hoping to make here!

I'm personally allergic to snobbishness.

Maybe we should have felt embarrassed or discouraged, but we didn't. Because that dichotomy fit us, and what we were trying to do. I'm personally allergic to snobbishness. It makes me cringe when people look down on what other people enjoy or wear, or when people view style as a sign of superficiality. I didn't have unlimited spending money growing up, but I loved fashion, and expressing my own personal style both made me a target and saved me from a life of people-pleasing and conformity. You know that scene in *Pretty Woman* where Vivian walks into the fancy boutique on Rodeo Drive and the salesgirls immediately decide she isn't worth waiting on? I wanted my jewelry to give women the exact opposite feeling. It matters to me—to us—that women feel worthy of something beautiful and something special. We could do that without the cost of an expensive booth put together by a production team. We could do it on our own, together, as a team.

It matters to me—to us—that women feel worthy
of something beautiful and something special.

We spent the next few days stepping out of our booth to sell however we could. Cheryl would stop Denise in an aisle and say loudly, "Oh, my gosh! I love that necklace! Where is it from?" And Cheryl would say, "Oh, it's Kendra Scott! They're nearly sold out! But maybe you can still get an order in if you're lucky." I'd stop buyers coming out of other booths and introduce myself, fully decked out in our favorite designs. If someone showed even a hint of interest, I'd take my necklace off and hand it to them with one of my business cards. We survived on the free snacks offered in the other brand booths, on the "free" lunch that came with our booth fee, and on the promise that when the doors closed, we'd all split a pizza from John's Pizza on Bleecker, to this day the best pizza in the world as far as I'm concerned. At night, we'd sit cross-legged on the beds hand-making the samples we hadn't finished. It was crazy, but *so* fun, and we fell asleep in our shared hotel room. We didn't have an HR department, and we also didn't have the cash for us to have our own rooms, let alone our own beds. We'd play rock, paper, scissors every night to see who got the bed and who ended up on the rollaway bed that was more like a cot. It was a sleepover and a business trip and a girls' trip all rolled into one, and in the early hours before the show began, we'd hightail it over to Kinko's to print up the line sheets we'd finished the night before. Nobody cared that our wallpaper was uneven and bubbly, and neither did we, especially after we tallied up our orders and realized that we'd hit 100K in immediate orders, fully liquidating our stock and getting us into boutiques and stores in time for the holidays. We'd done it! We flew back to Austin exhausted, elated, and with enough cash and new connections to keep our business going.

By late 2005, we'd officially outgrown our little attic office on Sixth Street. Not just the team of us who *worked* at Kendra

Scott Designs, but my kids, too. John and I had our second son, Beck, in 2004 and we couldn't scoot back our office chairs without knocking into one another, or a kid. None of us had a private office, but we'd converted a side storage room into a "nursery" for baby Beck. We'd made a mobile with tiny birds, put in a crib and a basket of toys, and made a little corner with a changing pad and wipes. As far as Beck knew, it was a dream room. But even with an air conditioner shoved into a window, all those people in a space that small made the room unbearably hot, and the front porch of the house-turned-commercial-space was always filled with our packages. But how could we leave? This was the first office we'd ever had, and we'd all screamed with joy when we saw our name go up on the dinky little sign on Sixth Street. This was where my babies had taken naps and practiced walking, it was where we got our first check from Nordstrom, which we'd nearly been so excited to see that I nearly forgot to deposit it. It's easy to romanticize the early days of anything—motherhood, a business, a relationship—but the early days of Kendra Scott were much different than the early days of the Hat Box. Ten years had passed since I started the Hat Box. I was older, wiser, and more grounded. I didn't set out to cure cancer or have a hundred stores or to prove anything to anyone: I wanted to make beautiful things with people I liked, and that's exactly what we were doing. But there was no denying that our little attic office was too small, and eventually, I had to walk downstairs and tell Mike, the best landlord in the world, we were moving out.

We both cried, but that's the thing about growth: it hurts. Our next space was a big, creaky warehouse with wide plank floors and plenty of room for us to spread out and make a little space for our kids to play and read while the moms worked. This was where Beck and Cade discovered their favorite game: hunting for gems between the cracks in the giant floorboards. Every wall was painted a different color—orange, yellow, green—and we added our own color with a design studio space that featured a big wall of acrylic bins filled with stones organized by color and by shape. For special events—a date, a big night out—the girls would use the design studio as their own personal accessory store, picking out colors and setting necklaces or earrings in a one-of-a-kind colorway just for *that* outfit.

While we were thriving and growing in our big new warehouse space . . . my marriage was falling apart. John and I had gotten married quickly, and had kids quickly (and close together), and we loved each other. I'd truly married a great guy, but my parents' marriage had shown me that even two good people can't always make a good marriage. But I was devastated and embarrassed. John wasn't just my husband and the father of my children, and his last name wasn't just my last name, it was a part of my brand. He was a well-known Austin businessman—still—and I was about to be his ex-wife . . . and we hadn't even made it a decade.

Nobody prepares you for the loneliness of a marriage ending; the person you've called your best friend, who you swore to be with until the end of your life . . . starts to feel like a stranger. A great distance opens up between you and the person you've slept next to for years, whose mind you swore you could read at some point. Marriage starts out with so much certainty: you know who will celebrate your birthday and help wrap Christmas presents. You know who to call when things are bad, or when you have great news. Divorce takes that certainty and replaces it with a series of unknowns. Who will be my emergency contact now? What will we do for Christmas? Who is going to end up with the dining room table? How can I live without tucking my kids in every single night?

It felt like the perfect life I'd worked so hard to create had become a snow globe that the universe had shaken without my permission. I was stuck in place while the pieces of my life I thought had been immovable were swirling around me. Compartmentalization kept me going. At work, I was calm and happy and focused. At home, I was calm and happy . . . until the boys went to bed and I was in bed alone and my naturally optimistic brain could only see the worst-case scenario. I'd cry until my eyes swelled shut, fall asleep to fitful dreams, and wake up to snuggle my boys and make them breakfast.

You can teach anyone a skill. What you can't teach is love, generosity, and kindness.

Cade was in school, and Beck had a part-time babysitter, but I still wanted to be the person to pick Cade up from school, to make the boys dinner, and tuck them in at night. I wanted to make sure that they felt like I did as a kid sitting in my dad's conference room or office while he went to court or took client meetings: that they were still a priority even if Mom had work to do. On the days they were with me, I focused on my work from 8:00 am to 2:00 pm, when I left the office and returned around 3:00 with my two favorite coworkers, who would color at the conference room table or hunt for gems between the floorboards. They were little, but they still remember these times together as happy days, totally oblivious to the kind of stress that was swirling around them, happy to be around their mom even if she was on a conference call. On the days they were with John, I'd work from the moment I opened my eyes until the minute I fell asleep (usually in bed with my laptop), so I wouldn't have to feel the pain of missing them and the life we'd had before.

While my personal life felt like it was one big rainy day, the energy in the office was sunshine and possibility. We read Simon Sinek's *Start with Why* and realized our *why* was obvious: joy. Maybe you thought I would have said jewelry, but no. It's *joy*. It's the feeling of watching someone open the perfect gift, of hearing a compliment when you least expect it. It's sunshine and friendship and laughter and *color*. It wasn't how our products made people look, but how it made them *feel*. I wanted our brand to spread joy and kindness with every interaction, the same way I want to make sure that my personal interactions do the same every day. For a customer, that means the kind of service that could make her jaw drop. In my life, it's meant going all out with holiday decorations, bringing in surprise breakfasts to the office, throwing birthday parties for my friends that take it up a notch every year. It's meant making eye contact and smiling at cashiers or buying coffee for a stranger or writing notes to tuck into the boys' backpacks. Joy creates joy, and we wanted every interaction with the brand to create a chain of joy a million miles long.

We were each other's inspiration, and random bursts of kismet seemed to punctuate our days. One day, I was excitedly explaining to Cheryl that a life coach I was seeing had given me a personality test from Insights Discovery based on four personality colors: red, blue, yellow, and green. I'd answered all the questions and eagerly awaited my results, which would give me insight into my management and communication styles. The coach blinked and recalculated the responses. She'd done hundreds of these tests and never seen someone come back with so much yellow. Yellow is the extrovert, the inspirer and encourager, and it was no surprise that nearly all of my answers reflected that. They called it, I told Cheryl, Sunshine Yellow.

"Yes!" Cheryl shouted into her computer monitor. "You're a yellow!"

"Right?" I said, ready to dive into what that could mean for our working relationship. But Cheryl was digging through her drawers for her Pantone swatch book.

"You're yellow! We're yellow!!!"

Successful women surround themselves with the friends who build them up and stand by them, no matter what.

She was tapping the page, and I saw it: our color. The brightest, most joyful yellow I'd ever seen. PMS 605C for the design nerds out there. That's how everything worked in those days; nobody got us like we got us and we had a near-telepathic level of communication. The *one* time we'd hired an outside design firm, they'd presented us with a logo that looked like a vulva, and we passed the assignment back to Cheryl. One of our most popular hoop earrings had a petal-like flourish at the end, and Cheryl had dragged an outline of the design into Illustrator and played with layering, making a pattern by locking them together in a cluster of four. It wasn't perfect, but she printed it up and left it on her desk while she moved on to some other work. I was zipping by her desk and stopped dead in my tracks.

"Cheryl!" I said, tapping at the center of the logo. "It's an evil eye!" I'd worn one on my wrist for years, a gift from my friend Roberta to protect my energy as we grew the company.

"Oh, my God, you're right." The logo that graces our bags and boxes and stores today is a variation of that first one I saw on Cheryl's desk.

The evil eye is still there, protecting the joy of everyone who carries it. The yellow is our signature color, a little bit of sunshine for anyone who sees it.

It took a long time to go from where we were to where we are, and even though the brand is my name, it holds the DNA of every person who was there in the earliest days, many of whom are still here today. Denise is our Senior Vice President of Customer & Creative, Cheryl is our Senior Vice President of Brand & Culture, and Leah is Senior Vice President of Design. Every one of those initial hires have developed far beyond the job they were first hired for, because you can teach anyone a skill. What you can't teach is love, generosity, and kindness. Every one of them made sure this little brand baby of mine had good genetic material, every one of them helped form the beating heart of the company. Not everyone stayed forever, but their impact remains, and we still maintain an amazing connection to this day. Should any of us need anything, we all know that our KS sisters and brothers would drop everything and show up. My mother always told me that your job as a parent is to give your children all the tools they need to fly out of the nest someday and soar. I believe that it's your duty as a leader to create other leaders. If that means people leave to follow their own dreams, great! I love nothing more than seeing previous Kendra Scott employees starting their own businesses and finding a life full of joy.

You do not need to do it all and you cannot do it all. Superwoman and Wonder Woman are fictional characters.

Outside of the office, I had a group of amazing friends who are still my chosen sisters to this day. Successful entrepreneurs surround themselves with people who know what they don't know and are experts in what they are not. Successful women surround themselves with the friends who build them up and stand by them, no matter what. We place a lot of emphasis on romantic relationships: on finding the right person, on getting married and having kids. And as a serial monogamist, I get it: I *love* love. I love my kids, and I love having a family. But when it all falls apart, your friends are going to be the ones who help you put it back together. When I became a single mom, many of them were still single, and they knew that if they wanted to see me, the boys would be tagging along. They'd join us for trips to the petting zoo or happy hours in the backyard, and made an effort to make sure I felt loved and supported even though our lives looked very different. A true friend wants you to win and wants to stand in the front row to cheer you on. If you're afraid to share the good stuff with your friends, if your friends make you feel like your ambitions aren't important, or your happiness is irritating . . . they might not be your friends, or at least not real, true friends. If we're lucky, life is long, and we'll meet a lot of people. As the saying goes, people enter your life for a reason or a season, and not every friendship is built to last the test of time or to make their way into your inner circle. There's no hard and fast rule or test to apply to your friendships to see which ones are worth it, which ones are right. There is only that internal antenna, a quiet sense of who is and is not your person. Listen to it. Listen to how you feel around people, to how you behave and act around them. Do you shrink yourself to fit their idea of you, do you put on a facade to fit in, or is being around them like slipping into cozy sweatpants and a T-shirt after a long day? Things change over the course of a friendship. You change. And a group friendship is a living, breathing organism in and of itself, an entire web of relationships that shift and change through the years. Not every friendship is meant for the long haul, but the longevity of any group isn't just kismet and luck: it's respecting and honoring the changes you've all been through, loving each other not just for who we've been for and to one another, but for the iterations you've been through over the years. However busy you are at this moment: stop. Put down this book. Pick up your phone. Call your friends and make a date. Keep it. Spend an hour together with your phones away, picking over cheap nachos or drinking on your couch. Share yourself and your life with them, and ask them about theirs.

Behind every successful woman is a whole community of people helping her, supporting her, reassuring her.

Having the dream is a one-woman job. Building and maintaining it takes a team. There is no way I would be who I am or where I am if I hadn't had a community of women to lean on and catch me when I was in the midst of a freefall, or to keep pushing me when the hill got steeper. You do not need to do it all and you *cannot* do it all. Superwoman and Wonder Woman are fictional characters, and the rest of us are out here thanking science for inventing dry shampoo so we can go one more day without having to wash *and* dry our hair. We tend to think of our lives as good times *or* bad times, but this period of my life showed me that it's often both, all at once. I let myself feel the pain of what I'd lost, but I never lost

Nine

Shaking the Snow Globe

Nobody opens a business expecting it to close. Nobody stands at an altar promising forever expecting to get a divorce. And nobody expects the entire economy to crumble beneath their feet right when they're gaining serious momentum. But these things happen: only 30% of businesses make it to the 10-year mark,[1] marriages end every day, and market crashes ruin lives, industries, and communities. Life is hard for everyone, and it's certainly not fair. Improv comedians use "yes, and" as their rule for the stage. This means that every actor who steps into a scene quickly accepts what is, and then adds to it. They don't walk onstage and say, "This isn't happening!" They walk on and continue the story. To me, that's what optimism feels like. I can walk into the reality of a situation, accept it . . . and see the possibility. And by 2008, everything felt possible. The pain of my divorce was now just a sore spot. John and I were now best friends and co-parenting like champions, and things at Kendra Scott were humming right along. We had our brand, our purpose, our vision, and what we stood for.

We were still a wholesale company, which meant that our relationship to our customers was nearly nonexistent. Our rep in Dallas—the one I'd been so nervous to meet a few years before—ran a showroom for buyers that featured several lines of jewelry. Buyers from big department stores and small boutiques would stop in to see what was new, and the orders flowed through the rep and down to whatever brands she'd sold through. Buyers loved us, so the arrangement worked out just fine . . . and besides that, this was just the way things were done. Unless you were a Tiffany or a Jared or some giant chain jeweler, this was the standard operating supply chain. Imagine a bustling warehouse filled with incoming orders of gems and raw materials, outgoing shipments for wholesale orders around the company, and desks of women designing and creating and cracking each other up all day . . . while Leah's baby is in a bouncy seat by her desk and the rest of our kids play in the corner.

That's what optimism feels like. I can walk into the reality of a situation, accept it . . . and see the possibility.

And then . . . the market crashed. All those investors who were only interested in websites and tech created a dot-com bubble that ended up bursting . . . and affecting *everyone*.

Nearly instantly, the bank called: they were pulling our line of credit. That line of credit was the cash flow that kept our business going and growing, and it was . . . gone. So were the buyers who loved our products; in what felt like one fell swoop we got emails announcing their layoffs. It didn't take long for the reality of the situation to set in: we had no relationship to our customers aside from spotting our designs out in the wild. That's thrilling, even today, but it wasn't going to cut it.

When the snow globe shakes, everything feels overwhelming and chaotic and *urgent*. I know from growing up in Wisconsin that in whiteout conditions, you pull the car over until you have some visibility. But we don't always have that privilege in life. Things won't stop just because we want them to, and the urgency I felt was real: it wasn't just my dreams that hung in the balance, it was the livelihoods of people I cared deeply about. There was no pulling over and waiting it out, it was time for action. Not reckless and reactive action, but smart, strategic action. Part of my "yellow" personality is that I'm spontaneous; when I get a vision, I see quickly not just what it is but how it comes together.

No business owner felt prepared for the 2008 crash, and I watched peers in other industries close up shop with a lump in my throat.

What I saw in the midst of this chaos was that relationships had been the key to my success so far: I got to know the small boutique owners who first carried my designs, and I kept strong relationships with our own vendors. But who was our customer? Where was our customer? And when the market came back, who would be the buyers that would fall in love with and stock our designs? One hundred percent of our revenue came through wholesale, which meant that there were at least three steps between us and our customers: **Kendra Scott • Rep • Buyer • Salesperson • Customer.** No business owner felt prepared for the 2008 crash, and I watched peers in other industries close up shop with a lump in my throat: I knew that kind of pain and wouldn't wish it on anyone. I also knew that the women who worked with me were in it with me, so I laid it all out on the table. I told them exactly how bad things were, and how much was at risk. I told them I was going to cut my pay even more, and I'd need some of them to do the same. If they couldn't do that, if they needed to leave, I wouldn't blame them a bit and I'd be the first person to write them a letter of recommendation for any job. But we needed to change our business model, and fast . . . or die right here and now. Not everyone could take that gamble, but many of them did, at immense risk to their own families. Our controller Christine went down to half-time just so we could keep her. This was a huge risk and a huge show of trust: there was no guarantee that this would work, but one by one, everyone agreed to jump off a cliff and help me build a plane on the way down.

It was the Great Recession, and while orders from our rep dried up, we spent hours around the conference room table trying not to succumb to the crushing sense of dread creeping in with every news report. I believe in following your dreams, but I did not expect to follow a *literal* dream. I burst into the conference room one day having woken up from what I was *sure* was the future for our company. I'd dreamed about what Denise and other employees sometimes did before dates or big events: taking extra stones and materials from our design space and setting a custom piece that perfectly matched their outfit. Our office was filled with women who were doing just that, but they weren't our employees . . . they were our customers. They were sampling from our acrylic bins like it was a jewelry salad bar and making the most gorgeous creations. In my dream, I'd asked where we were, and a woman smiled at me and said, "The Color Bar!"

I said all of this, rapid-fire, to the group of women who'd been by my side for years, and they *completely understood me*. Of course! The Color Bar! Cheryl was drawing up a logo in her sketchbook and Denise was talking about what the presentation would look like and Leah was on her feet thinking aloud with me about how it would work. Part of my dream was that we were at Henri Bendel, the premier accessories store in Manhattan, where Denise and Cheryl and I would go during our off times at the trade shows, dreaming about when we'd have our designs in this iconic store. I didn't have a contact there, but I picked up the phone and acted like the Color Bar was already the next big thing, and that they'd be lucky to have us.

Just a few months later, we were hauling boxes of heavy stones through the big, beautiful doors at Bendel's. We set up our most popular cuts organized by color in vintage candy dishes. We brought tools and gift boxes and yellow bags and set up shop for a three-day event. Around us, the recession was shuttering businesses left and right, but the line for the very first Color Bar—in New York City, no less—was *down the block*. And the line never let up either. The night was *incredible*, not just because we spent the night doing what we loved—making jewelry, chatting, and connecting with people—but because we got to see what our customers gravitated toward. Sales data is one thing, but seeing a real person react to your product is another. With all the options in front of them, it was clear which cuts were the favorite, and which gems. Some women came back three nights in a row, and the manager begged us to stay. We were there for three months, and the capital from that partnership kept us afloat financially and motivationally.

Next up, we needed a website. Okay, yes, we had a website, but we had never been a direct-to-consumer brand, so the website was purely informational: a contact form for interested wholesalers and a list of stockists for any consumer who straggled onto KendraScott.com. You couldn't buy anything from us directly, because I'd sworn off retail back when I closed the Hat Box. But hadn't that sign told me to stay open? Building an e-commerce website was a huge and potentially expensive undertaking: we were in a *recession*, were women really going to be getting online to buy themselves some new jewelry? There was only one way to find out. This website was a colossal undertaking in a world before SquareSpace and Shopify and all these amazing platforms that make it possible for people to establish their business online without ever hiring a web designer. We put the Color Bar front and center, and listed our standard products for sale directly to consumers for the first time. And then—just like that first day at the Hat Box—we waited for a customer. At least online nobody could see us waiting, refreshing our browsers until we saw it: our first sale. We screamed, and tried to resist spending the *entire day* refreshing. But we couldn't help it, it was so exciting! Everyone wanted to crowd into the "warehouse"—a glorified closet, really—to help pack and ship orders. We could see with our own eyes what was actually selling, not to boutiques, but to customers. It was nearly addicting, but it still wasn't enough. We needed to *know* our customer, and not just through an address and an order number. We needed a store. The entire economy was crashing around us—stores were closing left and right in our own town—but to paraphrase the poet Anaïs Nin, the day had come when the risk of staying in the bud was greater than the risk of blooming.

And so we bloomed. When the lease was up, we rented a two-story place on South Congress for an absolute steal. So many businesses had closed that South Congress was almost a ghost town, and we were the only ones who wanted the space. The downstairs would be a storefront, and the upstairs would serve as our office. South Congress was and is *the* street in Austin, the reason why people say Keep Austin Weird. And back then, it was even weirder: a mix of restaurants and clubs and shops with bright neon signs. The last time I'd owned a store, well, you know how it went. But this time I had a new vision: I wanted our customers to be invited in with the same warmth and grace that we'd offered women at Bendel's. I wanted it to be a place for women to gather, to experiment with their style, and to leave with a smile on their face whether or not they bought a single thing. I imagined it as a laboratory: our customers wouldn't be nameless, faceless women somewhere at the end of a supply chain, they'd be able to tell us face-to-face what they liked and didn't.

I had always hated the jewelry shopping experience, where you walk in and can feel a salesperson sizing you up to see what you can afford and if you're worth talking to. I didn't like having to ask to see things, or how every item was stored in glass cases. I understand loss prevention when you're talking about $10,000 bracelets, but why would I want to spend $100 at a store that doesn't trust me to look at a ring without supervision? I always felt afraid to ask for something, and afraid to turn something down, like I was subject to judgment if I didn't make a purchase. I'd rather not shop at all than shop at a place where I either felt pressured to buy something or ignored entirely. I wanted to foster an environment of *joy*, and there is no joy without trust. I envisioned a place where all of our designs were out in the open, where women could walk in and try something on without asking a salesperson to unlock a case, where you were greeted warmly and genuinely no matter what you were wearing or what you looked like. I wanted women to walk in and feel like they could relax, enjoy, and look around without feeling any pressure. I thought of that night at Bendel's, and how a group of strangers ended the night feeling like a group of friends. What if we held shopping parties where women could have a cocktail, hang out with their friends, and do a little shopping, *no purchase required*?

Not everyone understood the vision. People outside of our organization thought I was 100% crazy. They told me I'd lose a fortune to shoplifters, or go broke throwing parties for people.

My answer was always, "Okay!" Because I didn't believe it for a minute. I wasn't building a store for the 2% of bad people who, yeah, might swipe a necklace or two after grabbing a glass of free champagne. I was building a store for the 98% of good people. And we did. The very first Kendra Scott store opened in 2010 to a line snaking down South Congress as though Dolly Parton were playing a live show at the Paramount. Here, in real life, were the women who'd bought and gifted our jewelry, who'd begun to collect it for their own daughters and granddaughters. They streamed in for hours, and we watched our vision come to life. The Color Bar was no longer a trunk show at Bendel's, it was a permanent fixture in a real store with my name on it. It was a warm, welcoming environment for women to create their own pieces from the classic design elements Kendra Scott was known for: bright semi-precious stones in signature cuts you couldn't get anywhere else, and quality metals and finishes. Women could come in, design a beautiful piece of jewelry . . . and have a cupcake and a glass of champagne. What could be better? The layout of the space was perfect for what we wanted: walking in the door, you were in a bright, sunny storefront. Walk to the back of the store, and a staircase led up to a lofted office space, with real offices and a conference room and a little kitchen . . . and no shag carpeting. When we stepped out for lunch, we had to walk through the store—which opened at 10:00 am—and right onto the sales floor.

We'd stop and chat with bridal parties looking for necklaces to match their dresses, or moms shopping for a grad gift for their daughters, and chat with the sales team about what was selling and what wasn't. As weeks went by, we started to get a sense of who our customers really were, and design with them in mind. We'd had no idea how many of our customers were schoolteachers, or new moms, or nurses. Everything we learned about these women provided endless inspiration: a special discount for teachers, supporting nonprofits focused on literacy and education, 50% off a piece of jewelry as a birthday gift. Our focus was always on how we could serve her and what was important to her, how we could make her feel seen and appreciated. And to this day, we still think a glass of champagne and a cupcake helps.

Entrepreneurs are always telling aspiring businesses that they need to be disruptive . . . because it's true. Sometimes that disruption is literal: the Blue Man Group started as a group of friends in blue masks who led a street procession through Central Park.[2] Now they've performed internationally for millions of people. Every market feels overcrowded until you can figure out what makes you different. We didn't paint ourselves blue, but the choices we made were disruptive to the industry from the beginning, from the colors and stones we used to letting our shoppers custom-create their own jewelry at the Color Bar to giving them 50% off an item for their birthday . . . all of the choices that are core to our brand made us disruptors, outliers. An e-commerce website is basic table stakes now, but I cannot emphasize enough how risky this all was at the time: direct sales meant directly managing individual orders, which meant reconfiguring our warehouse and distribution model, establishing a customer relationship management system (CRM), establishing customer service protocols to interface with any customer issues, marketing directly *to* our customers . . . the list went on and on. These two choices—opening a store and establishing our e-commerce site—spun into literally hundreds of additional decisions and increased our risk significantly. They have also been key to our survival, and our lightning-in-a-bottle growth. Forget a plane, we had a rocket ship now.

———

When I established the business in 2002, wholesale was 100% of our business. In 2022, it's 15% of our overall business. I don't think that we'd have closed during the crash if we hadn't pivoted the business to direct to consumer, but we certainly wouldn't have been able to grow to where we are now. We'd have made significant lay-offs and cutbacks, and we'd have had to wait for our reps to establish new relationships with new buyers. We'd have plugged along and survived, but we wouldn't have thrived without asking this question:

What's the worst that could happen?

I know I called myself an optimist—and I am—but in both my divorce from John in 2006 and the crash of 2008, I allowed myself to think through the absolute worst-case scenario, to let my most anxious thoughts tell me a story, then let myself sit with the absolute worst feeling I could imagine: I'd see myself closing the doors of Kendra Scott and laying off the team, liquidating all of the inventory and handing over every piece of personal property to the banks who had required them as collateral. I'd see myself selling the house my boys had come home to from the hospital, and living with my mother, my sister, my friends. I'd feel the very real sense of disappointment, shame, and fear. My throat would tighten, my cheeks would turn red, and I'd let myself cry as though it were really happening. Like, really cry, as hard as I needed to. And when I was done, I'd feel a sense of clarity and peace: *okay, that's it. That's what it would feel like. Not forever, but at least for a while.* But right now? None of that is true yet, and I can feel something else and *do* something else. I can take action from where I am right now, not where I'm afraid I might end up.

The optimist in me is not going to tell you to *not be afraid.* Any person who claims to be fearless is actually foolish. Rob survived two tours in Vietnam as a very young man, and he lived every day of his service in the very real fear that he would lose his life, or one of his fellow servicemen. Our family was afraid to lose Rob—and we did. The very worst-case scenario came true, and still, we survived. And after that divorce, I did end up moving out of that house . . . and I found a cute little rental to make into a home for me and the boys.

The optimist in me is going to tell you that fear is not your enemy, but your friend. Every moment of dramatic, positive forward change in my life has come from fear: I was afraid to move to Texas, afraid to close the Hat Box after Rob died, afraid of divorce, afraid to dramatically change our business model. And I didn't avoid fear, I leaned into it. I asked questions like *what are you afraid will happen?* I listened and asked *okay, then what?* Once I'd let myself go to the scariest place, I knew that I could survive it. Your fear is a smaller, scared version of yourself. Don't ignore her, *listen to her.* Accept exactly where you are in this moment, and move forward . . . together.

When you're in it—a divorce, a job loss, whatever shakes your snow globe—it feels like this might be forever. We know intellectually that it isn't true, that all things must pass, but try to tell that to a person who just spent forty minutes signing what feels like a thousand pieces of paper saying, "You are not married anymore." Motion does not need to be perpetually *forward*, and it can't be. Nature proves to us every year that there are times for growth, and times for rest. A lateral move—or no move at all—is sometimes exactly what you need. When the snow globe shakes, please know that where you are now is just where you are now, and whatever part of your identity is being stripped away will be replaced with something else. When it all settles, you could have something stronger, something truer, something meant to last, and maybe something that was always there.

Ten

The Billion-Dollar Seat

alt Whitman said that we contain multitudes, but my dad, Ken, *lives* in those multitudes. Dad wasn't just a cowboy lawyer who also did my laundry and took me shopping, he was a self-taught photographer who spent his off-hours cataloging the world around us through his own unique lens. A lot of people who grew up in the eighties are blessed with boxes of awkward childhood photos taken on film, but I'm blessed with boxes of magazine-worthy candids that my father developed in the basement "darkroom" he constructed on his own. Sure, he *could* have taken his rolls of film to the local photo shop to have them developed and printed, but where's the fun in picking up the finished product when you can instead spend weeks processing the film, selecting your favorite negatives, and developing them into a real photograph?

Stepping into Dad's DIY darkroom was like stepping into a magic trick: chemistry, artistry, intuition, and routine brought his visions to life in front of me. If anything was off—the temperature, the developer, the water—it didn't work, but Dad wasn't precious about anything. He'd pull up a stool in front of his workspace and let me help him move the blank piece of paper from tray to tray until images materialized in front of us: my mother's laughing face, my classmates and I lined up for swim lessons, my grandparents posed on their sofa. He let me adjust the color or the contrast, and we'd talk through what we liked in the images we were creating, and why. He could have reserved this just as "his" time, but he let me in, and let me make mistakes and witness his own. Film photography is a finicky art. When it was time, we'd carefully hang them from the clothesline that ran the length of the room and let them dry, creating a tiny museum of our family memories. Dad's brain was filled with laws and statutes and briefs and trial details, but he always had room for more: photography used a different part of his brain and his spirit.

Whether by genetics or osmosis, I have the same duality in me: my left and right brains are equally active, if not always at the same time. It's probably not a coincidence that every entrepreneurial endeavor I've followed has been rooted in style and fashion; I can get lost in color, pattern, and design one day, and pore over a P&L statement the next. And yes, I'm a college dropout, but I love to learn. From the moment I started the Hat Box, I was a regular at the local library, checking out books on leadership and business and trying to soak up any kind of wisdom I could. Entrepreneurship is lonely, even when you're lucky enough to have the kind of team I've built and the group of friends I have. Because when it comes down to it, the success or failure of your venture comes down to you, and when other people are counting on the business to help them pay their mortgage or their kids' tuition or, heck, even buy their weekly groceries, that's nothing to take lightly. I would have loved an MBA—and the network that comes with it—but I was busy with the boys and a growing business, and I didn't have the time to pour myself into a program. By 2006, the business was doing over a million dollars in revenue, and I couldn't shake the feeling that we were on the precipice of something bigger. You know the feeling you get as the roller coaster climbs that first hill, and you see the ride spread out in front of you? It felt like that, like anything could happen, like this idea that investors had dismissed just a few years before was exactly what I knew it could be: great.

Investors interested in tech may not have seen the potential of a joy business *or* a jewelry business, but the Texas business community took me in and gave me a seat at the table long before I had stores around the country. Steve Hicks is a Texas business legend, a radio man who bought his first radio station before he had even turned thirty. His business couldn't have been more different than mine, but we were an instant match in our enthusiasm and energy, and he became my friend and my mentor. Every day I woke up running a company bigger than it was the day before, and that's still true today. The only way to navigate uncharted territory is to find people who have been there before. So many people are scared to ask for help, thinking it's a sign of weakness to expose that they don't know everything. Of *course* you don't know everything, but when you're clear about what you need to know and reach out to a person you admire with a specific ask? Nine times out of ten, they'll be happy to help. Show up prepared—even to a phone call—and respect the other person's time by knowing exactly what you need. I didn't have a board, but I wanted people to report to, so I reached out to people I admired to form an advisory board. I couldn't afford to pay anyone, but I knew their time had immense value, so I reached out to three people I admired to see if they would take an earned-in-equity position. In exchange for their time in a quarterly check-in, I gave them a small stake in the company. One was a woman who'd built several retail brands into international powerhouses. One was a tech guy who could help me expand our e-commerce capabilities. The other was Steve, an incredible businessman and philanthropist. Steve was a sounding board for me: he'd been in every room I walked into, and the ones I hadn't dreamed of visiting yet. He refused the earned-in-equity position, but he did become my first investor. Steve was the person who suggested I join the Entrepreneurs' Organization (EO), an international networking group of entrepreneurs from across every industry you could imagine. Here were people who were wired like me: to see possibility and embrace risk and build a plane while flying it. The program connected us with mentors and with each other, and you probably know from your own experiences that connecting with a person who shares a similar life experience can be transformational. The EO network meant that I had an outlet for roadblocks and conundrums that weren't appropriate to put on my team, my husband, or my friends. It meant access to other founders and incredible opportunities.

The Entrepreneurs' Organization Entrepreneurial Masters Program at MIT is highly selective: to apply, you need to be the founder of a business clearing one million in revenue, and even then, the program accepts only sixty-eight participants . . . from around the world. Instead of the two-year full-time commitment of an MBA, the group meets once a year for three years, in four-day intensive workshops, learning from the kinds of people whose books were on our shelves and whose accomplishments we had only dreamed of. I'd heard that John Mackey of Whole Foods had gone through this program, that their objective was to find the next Steve Jobs or Richard Branson. I felt silly filling out the application—an echo of the reactions I'd heard in my first investor pitches—but I sent it off anyway. *Couldn't hurt to try*, I thought as I clicked Submit and left the office for daycare pickup. But I got in. I got in, and a few weeks later, I was on a plane with my most serious business outfits ready to meet the group of entrepreneurs who had the same big dreams I did.

The first day of "school" as an adult was even more nerve-wracking than middle school, but when I walked into that lecture hall . . . it only got worse. The room was filled with founders in different sectors, from different parts of the globe, each of us facing our own unique challenges. I had thought I'd feel excited walking in, but instead I felt like Elle Woods in *Legally Blonde* . . . because in this entire group, there were only four women in the room. Four! Instantly, I regretted applying and regretted attending. Was I just a quota they needed to fill? A way to show that this wasn't just a boys' club? I took a seat in the very back of the room, cracked the spine of the brand-new notebook I'd brought for the occasion, and got ready to learn. Our group leader—Brian—stepped up to say a few words before we got started, and while I'm sure he said many inspiring things, the sentence that stuck in my head was this:

"One of you is sitting in a billion-dollar seat."

We all looked around to see who it was: The AI guy from Australia? The algorithm guy from India? The *other* tech guy from Germany? In the next three years, EO was sure that at least one of us was going to make it big.

Our days were twelve or more hours scheduled down to fifteen-minute increments, and on the first day, I was lost. There were so many acronyms I hadn't even heard yet: EBITDA? COGS? CSF? DSF? It felt like everyone was speaking in code, and I had to wait to get to my hotel room to look up the answers later because my BlackBerry barely got service, and besides, we were supposed to be avoiding any outside distractions.

By Day 2, I was slightly more comfortable, but I stayed in my seat in the back of the room while Cameron Herold, known as the CEO Whisperer, took to the stage and walked us through an exercise he called Vivid Visions. Opening my notebook, I listened while he described what we were doing: creating our vision for three years into the future of our company. Imagine, he told us, jumping into a time machine and traveling three years into the future of your business and describing it for your colleagues back in the past. On the screen behind him were a series of bullet points, a guide for where to start. The instructions were clear:

- Write as though everything has already happened. You don't need to describe *how* it happened, just what *is*.

- As if you're walking around your office and stores, you describe:
  - The energy you feel.
  - The way the employees are working with each other.
  - How your core values are being lived.
  - You describe sales.
  - You describe marketing.
  - You describe PR.
  - You describe operations.
  - You describe customer service.
  - You describe IT.
  - You describe finance.
  - You describe how you work with your accountants, lawyers, and advisers.
  - You write about what the media is saying about you and the company in the press.
  - You write about what your customers are writing about you on Google and Yelp.
  - You write about what your employees are writing about you on Glassdoor and Indeed.
  - You describe your meetings.

You write down every aspect of your company as if it has already come true, and in the end, you have a Word document that's about four pages long. We turned ours in to Cameron—who promised to email them to us in three years—and brought a copy back to our offices. It was our job to create the vision and to let our teams help make it come true.

Cameron travels the world teaching this method, and because he's now a dear friend and mentor, he let me share it with you in this book. I can't tell you anything else that happened in that room, because a key component to the program is confidentiality; anything said within those walls stays there. But the vulnerability I saw within that space proved to me that the challenges and issues that I'd faced in business were far from unique. Maybe you already figured this out, but I was the person sitting in that billion-dollar seat. I teach in that same room now, and I tell my story to a group of nervous and optimistic entrepreneurs, and I always point at whoever sits in that seat in the back. The seat didn't magically turn the company into a billion-dollar brand, we did that: with our team, with our board of advisers, and with Steve, who later became my very first investor and calls me his bonus daughter. When Cameron sent me my Vivid Visions document three years later, everything I'd written *was* true.

We were not an overnight success, and nobody ever is. Most of us are like the photos that my father developed in our basement darkroom, the result of patience and curiosity and the right formula at the right time. It's worth all of the patience and persistence—all of the trial and error—to see what develops.

Eleven

What Matters to You?

In the early days of building Kendra Scott, I was told that there was no way I'd make it as a designer. It was cute and all that I started a business out of my spare bedroom in Texas, but to really make it, I'd need to be based in New York or Los Angeles. That was never going to happen: I love visiting both of those cities, but Texas was and always will be my home. I refused to believe that the only path to success meant changing who I was. If I hadn't folded under the pressure of middle school, a few investors weren't going to change my mind.

My personal brand and my actual brand aren't all that different. Because a brand is not just the perfect logo or the right color (although those are crucial elements, and Cheryl *nailed* it on both counts). A brand is what you do and why you do it, a reflection on the people who created it and who support it. I've known since I was a little girl exactly who I was, and I had a team who was willing to roll up their sleeves and help create my vision. That said, the branding process was not all smooth sailing. I told you about the vulva logo, but did you know that our first brand color was . . . periwinkle? And I don't even like purple! But there were some elements of the brand process that came easily. Every brand should have a set of core values: principles that guide their decision-making and are reflected in the way they show up in their industry and their community. People have them, too, even if they don't realize it.

Our core values as a brand became crystal clear as soon as we set aside time as a group to talk about what was important to us. It's such a simple question, and one we so rarely have the time to think deeply about. You could probably make a quick list of what you value, but have you ever had the time to think deeply about why you value it, and how that value shows up in your life? We took a whole business day away from our to-do lists and our emails and our meetings and talked about what was important to us as people and as a business.

What did we love? Nearly everyone in the office was a young mother—every one of our kids had spent time playing at the office while their mom worked—and we all wanted to have a career *and* a family. Where other companies saw mothers as liabilities who might need to cut out of work early for kid pick-up or doctor's appointments, we see each other as assets, and never wanted to feel as though we had to sacrifice one for the other. We wanted our customers to feel that way, too. We created something we called the Sister Rule. How would you treat your sister if she walked into the store with a broken earring? How would you *want* her to be treated by someone else? Well, you'd fix her earring or give her a 50% discount on a replacement pair. You wouldn't insist on seeing a receipt or asking a manager, you'd do it.

Then we started to talk about what we love to do. We were Texas girls who loved fashion and design and making things that make women feel beautiful. Fashion isn't shallow, it's a form of art. The art that we create helps us and other women show the world who we are. It's self-expression and self-love. We wanted to give that to every woman at a price she could afford, to create something beautiful for her that wouldn't cost her an entire paycheck.

We were driven and passionate, but success for us was about the kind of impact we could have in our community. We'd been giving away jewelry to any charity that called since day one, but we had a vision to fund the initiatives that supported the social issues we cared deeply about: women and children's charities that focus on health, education, and empowerment.

The process of developing the brand of Kendra Scott had a surprising effect on me: it gave me a lot of clarity on who I was as a person. I was *me*. That sounds simple, but we live in a culture that is obsessed with the "personal brand," and where people seem to think that means creating an image that looks better than their reality. I'm a designer and I love fashion, so I'm not knocking anyone who likes to look good, but style needs substance and there's nothing more substantial than the truth. At Kendra Scott, we believe that the customer is our boss. She signs the checks, and it's our job to continue to wake up every day to surprise and delight her, to meet her with joy and kindness, whether that's in our store or online. That's a reflection on how I live my life, too. I want to create a brand that leaves a legacy of kindness and joy, and raise a family that does the same long after I'm gone. When I'm asked for branding advice—and sometimes even when I'm not—I tell people to be honest. To be who they are. Anyone can sniff out a phony, and nobody likes a faker. A lot of the people you see posting on Instagram and talking about their personal brand are faking it, posting photos in a rented jet, showing you their expensive bags but not their mountain of credit card debt.

Brands do this, too. To prove they've "made it," they'll open their first store on the flashiest street in the most expensive cities. Will the store make money? No, it might bleed them dry. But at least it looks good. We did this. The second store we opened was in Beverly Hills just off Rodeo Drive. We thought we needed it to build recognition, but it didn't work. Why? It wasn't authentic. We weren't a Beverly Hills brand, and we were out of step with our values and our brand story. Some brands have to make up a story for themselves. You can tell, because it sounds like it was written in a game of Marketing Department Bingo. Just like with people, nobody likes a phony. You don't need a better story or a better version of your life. You are who you are. You came from where you came from. That's exactly what makes you who you are. I've said before that the minute a brand tries to do what everyone else is doing, they've already failed. Was I the first person to ever make jewelry? Of course not! But I had custom shapes, custom filigree, and customer service that set us apart from any competitor. We didn't create from a template, but from what set us apart. This goes for people, too. You don't need to do what everyone else is doing to find success, happiness, or peace. Your life and your story are uniquely yours. Why waste it trying to be someone else?

Being clear on your core values is like lining up the foundation of who you are. The core values of family, fashion, and philanthropy have guided our company to heights we couldn't have imagined. And they've guided me, too. Whenever I've been in a friendship, a relationship, or even a business deal that feels off, it's been a sign that the situation is not aligned with who I am. Your personal core values are in you, and you can find them with a few questions:

- What in life brings you joy?
- What in life brings you peace?
- How would you want people to describe you?
- What are the things in life that make you angry? Upset?
- What are the most important parts of your life?
- What are the things you cannot live without?
- What are the things that you'd do anything to avoid?

Ask the people who know you best—your partner, your best friends—what they think your core values are. What words come to mind when they think of you and how you live and work? Do the words they come up with align with what you've written? Your personal core values are yours, but you might benefit from having a conversation about them with the people close to you. First, they might not even know what's truly important to you. And second, imagine how much deeper your relationship might get if they have this information. Nobody can tell you what your core values are—what's really important to you—but the people closest to you are your mirrors, and they can tell you if you're really living up to them . . . or not.

Knowing what I value has also given me a good radar for what *other* people value. Not everyone in your life has to be exactly like you—your personalities and interests can be wildly different—but your inner circles should be people whose values complement your own. You don't need replicas of yourself. We need people around us with different talents and traits and passions. But you need to surround yourself with people who share your heart. Personality-wise, opposites attract. Values-wise? It's never going to work. When you know who you are, you don't just know what you want, but what you don't.

It's a noisy world out there, filled with distractions and demands. The power of core values is not to give you *rules* to live by, but to remind you of who you are and what matters.

Twelve

We Do Good

osing Rob wasn't my first experience with cancer. When I was in sixth grade, my friend Katie's mom got sick. She had been the leader of our Brownie troop in elementary school, the kind of woman who lights up a room with her energy, who seems to always have a smile on her face and something baking in the oven. Being around her as a little girl was like stepping into sunshine: she made you feel as though you were the center of her world, even if there were twelve other little girls begging for her attention. Nobody explained to us what breast cancer was, or where it came from. Nobody told us what Katie's mom was going through, or what would happen next. But we could tell that it wasn't good, that her vibrant light was being dimmed. Katie got quieter at school, and when I went to her house her mother didn't always have the energy to greet us in the kitchen with after-school snacks. She'd be resting in her room, and Katie and I would play quietly in the living room, trying not to disturb her mother or mention the elephant in the room: Katie's mom was dying.

I am not a person who hates hospitals: I know from experience that they are places of hope and healing, where people show up every day to dedicate their lives to the care and curing of other human beings. But I do hate what cancer takes from people, how it robs people of their identity and turns them into Sick People. Katie's mother was not just a sick person, she was a person. And though I never got the chance to know her as an adult, the woman I knew as a child was a person who brought color to my world and my life, especially when my own mother had moved away.

To some people, it sounded crazy: you want to make jewelry . . . in a hospital? Don't you think these people have bigger things to think about? But we knew it wasn't crazy, and we knew it wasn't trivial: everyone craves beauty and joy, especially when they're facing the darkness. Art and creativity had saved me when I was a little girl playing dress-up in my aunt Jo Ann's closet, and art was paying the bills for every woman who worked with me. Art was what women bought from us and wore proudly in good health and in bad. I'd been told by an investor once that artists didn't make good businesspeople because we were too concerned with how things looked to pay attention to how they worked. I thought of him every time we shipped an order or collected an invoice, and I could imagine what he'd say if I'd told him I was planning to go to a hospital and give our product away to any woman who wanted it . . . he'd probably blow a gasket. But I know there is magic in creativity and art, in creating something with your own hands even if they are shaking. And after a tour of the pediatric cancer floor at MD Anderson, I wanted to do something to bring joy to these children, their mothers, and the people who care for them. What if . . . we brought the Color Bar to them? We reached out and told them we'd follow any health protocols they asked for, do any background check, jump through any hoop it took: we just wanted to spread some joy.

Giving was not standard business practice when I started the Hat Box, or when I started Kendra Scott, but it's always been a part of my business.

A few weeks later, we were walking through the doors of MD Anderson for our first Kendra Cares event. We didn't have a big strategy or even a fully operationalized plan: we just knew that we wanted to show up with what we had—gems and settings—and spread some joy. We hauled in heavy boxes of our best-selling gems and reassured everyone who asked us that, yes, we were here to give away our jewelry and, no, there was no catch. That first day, we followed nurses into quiet rooms and sat at bedsides, helping patients create the necklace, bracelet, or earrings they wanted. We sat with young girls and teenagers and with their mothers. Together, we sorted through the stone shapes and colors, picked metals, and created a final product that made them smile. I couldn't tell you what that day cost us, but I can tell you we all walked out of the hospital that day knowing that this was a permanent part of the business, that we were only getting started.

Months after that first Kendra Cares event, I got an email. I mean, I get a lot of emails but this one was from a teenage girl who'd been at the hospital the first day we stopped in. She'd made herself and her mother necklaces with a coral pendant, her favorite color, and they'd worn them every day of her treatment. Now that it was over, they wore them as a reminder that they deserved good things. It was a thank you email, but the gratitude I felt reading it was immeasurable.

My mother had taught me that if someone complimented anything three times, you should give it to them on the spot.

Giving was not standard business practice when I started the Hat Box, or when I started Kendra Scott, but it's always been a part of *my business*. I'm happy to say that today, most businesses have realized that doing good is just as important as doing well. But before I had that meeting with my rep in Dallas, before I was in any major store, I was always giving things away. My mother had taught me that if someone complimented anything three times, you should give it to them on the spot. I'd find myself taking the earrings out of my ears at school pickup, or unfastening my necklace at the grocery store, thrilled to be able to make someone's day and outfit a little more beautiful. I said yes to every charity that asked for items for their silent auction, even when they wanted my more expensive pieces. A lot of people warned me against this: they told me I'd go broke, that donations hardly ever translated into sales, that I was giving away my money and my product and would regret it. Well, I haven't yet.

My parents and their parents were the kind of people who would give you the coat off their backs even in the thick of a Wisconsin winter. Not because it would end up as a viral video, but because it's the right thing to do. By the time I was in fifth grade, my mother was one of the top Mary Kay reps in our region, and I was her faithful assistant. I rushed home from school every day to set up shop next to her in the small office my father had made for her in what used to be a utility room. It was here, in just a few square feet, where my mother lovingly filled each of her orders. She could have just driven through town dropping cardboard boxes in people's mailboxes, but instead I stood next to her watching her elegant hands write out personalized notes on thick cardstock, placing even the smallest orders in a gift bag bursting with tissue paper and fastened with a bow of ribbon that she curled between her thumb and the open blade of a scissor.

She explained to me that we never know what's going on with another person, that the woman who placed this order could be having a hard day, a hard week, a hard *life*. This package could be a bright spot that lights her up, and opening it should feel like releasing a butterfly. My mother knew many of the people she was selling to personally, but she treated every potential customer as a *person*. If someone wasn't in the market for the new lipsticks or didn't have the budget for a new powder, my mother would still send her home with samples—a lotion, a face wash, a perfume—packaged as if she'd placed the biggest order possible. These women weren't just numbers on a balance sheet, they were people: teachers and mothers and sisters with their own stories and their own lives. Mom gave freely and without an ulterior motive, driving around the greater Kenosha area delivering little bags of joy to everyone she could.

The day we opened that first Kendra Scott store, I hugged and shook hands with people who told me they'd never forgotten what we gave for their silent auction or fundraiser years before. I'd never expected to have those kindnesses repaid, but here they were, standing in line for hours to show up for our little store. Having a brick-and-mortar location gave us a whole new world of possibilities. We started with Kendra Gives Back, where anyone could host a shopping event with 20% of each sale going back to the charity of their choice. We provided champagne and music, the host sent the invites, and the donations grew from a few hundred dollars at a time to a few thousand.

People want to work for people who care, who walk the walk, and who invest in their communities.

Above: Expressing myself through fashion at a
young age . . . check out all the accessories!

Below: Me and Grandpa Dick.

Above: Yellow-colored glasses back in the Kenosha days.
Below: With my dad in the Stickster days . . . I did my best to rock that hair!

Above: Modeling the merch at the Hat Box.

Below: My mom in her Mary Kay days.

Above left: Me and Rob. Look at that tan!
Above right: Me and Ashlynn living it up in Austin.
Below: With Holley, my angel and inspiration.

With Denise (left) and Cheryl in the early days of Kendra Scott.

Above: My mom, me, and all my amazing siblings!

Right: Just the three of us: Cade, Beck, and me post-divorce.

Below: My miracle baby Grey at a store opening.

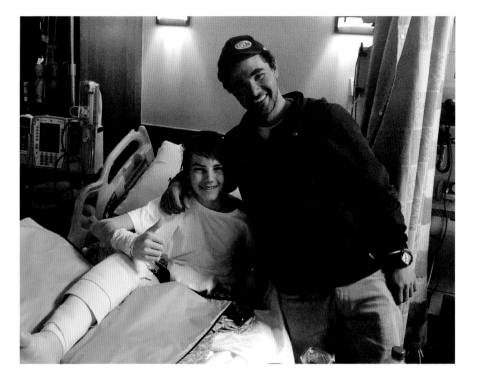

Above: Beck with our hero, Damian.

Below: All my babies . . . growing up too fast!

Duke, the love of my life.

Before I'd even made a dollar, Rob had told me "you do good." He meant it as words of encouragement, but it's now a directive in my life, a part of the core values for myself and for the company. Our giving has grown alongside our business, as part of the three pillars of this business: family, fashion, and philanthropy. And I don't say this to brag, though I'm very proud of it. I say this because success cannot just be limited to the bottom line. Very few people are energized by or inspired to work with companies whose only purpose is growth. A study by Deloitte[1] found that purpose-driven companies have a 40% higher retention rate, and employee turnover is one of the highest costs of doing business. Bottom line: people want to work for people who care, who walk the walk, and who invest in their communities. It doesn't just feel good (though, yes, it does feel great), it makes good sense. The investors who told me I was foolish for giving away my product were fools themselves.

Nearly two decades later, we can show the impact that Kendra Gives Back events have on our communities. These events can be hosted by our customers or local organizations in any of our stores or online: it's a social shopping experience where 20% of sales will go to the nonprofit of your choice. In just the last four years, we've hosted over 30,000 giveback events across the country supporting local causes. Since 2015, we've given out over $27 million in cash donations and $31 million in in-kind donations to community organizations supporting women and children in the areas of health and wellness, education, entrepreneurship, and empowerment. We've hosted events for over 30,000 charities and individuals in need. We've touched the lives of over

20,000 pediatric patients and caregivers through our Kendra Cares Mobile Color Bar across 40 hospitals nationwide. We've provided 4.3 million meals to families in need. And we have funded close to 21,000 hours of research against metastatic breast cancer.

For years, we had a giant thermometer in our corporate office that we'd fill in with markers to measure our giving for the year. When we set a 3 million dollar goal for Kendra Gives Back events one year, we took that number as seriously as we did topline revenue. Our store managers knew that giving was a key performance indicator and a measure of their—and our—success. We have big corporate giving initiatives, but it's a high priority for our giving to reflect what's important to each individual community, and to empower our teams to get out there and give. While I am writing this, a store manager heard about a terrible car accident in her community, where a mother lost three of her four children and was badly injured herself. Within a week, the team had contacted the family and local media and put together a Kendra Gives Back event to assist the family with medical bills.

Before you close this book and think you need to give away every dollar you make: stop. Not everyone is able to write a big check or fund a huge research grant, I know. Before we could give at this scale, we gave what we could: a necklace for a silent auction, an hour of my time for a young business student, volunteer hours at the organizations that touched our hearts. Whatever you can give has immense value, no matter the dollar value attached to it. Give what you can, when you can, and know that all of it counts, all of it matters.

Thirteen

Average Family

In the eighties, we called families like mine "broken homes." The term was so ingrained in our culture I never bothered to question it, but every time I heard it on the news or in school, it stung. And no wonder! Nobody wants to be broken, nobody wants to feel as though their family is less than another. My parents' divorce was painful for me, but spending time with my dad in our little condo—or with my mom in Chicago—didn't feel broken. It felt normal. It wasn't what I chose, but it *was* what I had.

I know lots of people in my generation who grew up in divorced families and swore that they would *never* get a divorce. I was one of those people, but aren't we all on our wedding day, and in the years and months and days leading up to it? Most people enter marriage optimistically, but an *optimist* enters a marriage with a kind of certainty in their current and future good fortune. I just *knew* when I walked down the aisle toward John that I was walking toward my forever.

Well. You know how that turned out.

Getting divorced sucks. I've done it more than once, and so far . . . it hasn't gotten any easier. For people aching for the juicy details of my marriages and divorces, I'm sorry to say you won't find them in these pages. The stories are the same as any other you've heard: two people tried, and it didn't work. The details are irrelevant, and I'm not saying that to be coy, but to respect the privacy of people I once loved. Each of these relationships taught me something and gave me something, even if it took me years to figure out what those lessons and gifts were.

Divorce is disorienting, painful, expensive, and for many of us . . . shameful.

Every time I've said "I do" I meant it; I saw myself growing older with this person, sitting side by side on a couch watching our grandchildren open Christmas presents. Every time it became obvious that forever was going to be a lot shorter than I'd anticipated, I felt the same crushing ache in my chest, the floor falling away below me, a loss of an identity and a life plan. Divorce is disorienting, painful, expensive, and for many of us . . . shameful. How could we promise 'til death do us part and yet be out here alive and in different houses, living separate lives? There is no feeling like feeling you've let down your children, and I was sure that I had done just that. Now my own kids would have to have two Christmases and two bedrooms, would have entirely different families and traditions and rules about bedtime and screen time. This was not the plan.

To show up ready and willing to brave the risk of heartbreak when your best laid plans have been decimated is gutsy and admirable.

For all that's changed in the decades since my own parents' divorce, the shame around ending a marriage has not, especially when there are kids involved. So many of us—myself included—are disappointed that we couldn't provide our kids with a standard Average Family. But what exactly is average, and why do we want it? If it's 2.5 kids and a house in the suburbs with a picket fence, it might comfort you to know that *that* family is actually not average at all. According to Pew Research, there *is* no Average Family anymore. Most families are made up of all kinds of configurations that don't fit into the "typical" mold we were all trying to form ourselves into. There's a lot of judgment around divorce and remarriage, a judgment that doesn't seem to apply to people who have other monogamous relationships that *aren't* legally binding. It's strange to me, because I see it as a choice that reflects the bravery it takes to love. Love itself is a huge risk; it opens you up to new levels of joy and pain. To show up ready and willing to brave the risk of heartbreak when your best laid plans have been decimated is gutsy and admirable. It was courageous of my mother to start over as a divorced young woman with three kids in the 1960s. She was an outlier in a community of nuclear families, including her family of origin. It was brave of my father to marry her and raise my sisters as his own blood. Without my parents bucking tradition and breaking the mold, I wouldn't have my sisters, I wouldn't have had Rob and the two sons who became my little brothers. I wouldn't have the life I have and love without the lives my parents lived separately *and* together, and neither would my own children.

At John's house, Beck and Cade have two little sisters from their dad's second marriage, two little girls who light up a room and light up their big brothers' lives. At my house, they have Grey, a funny, feisty, hilarious little brother who thinks he has the two coolest brothers in the world. Grey was almost an impossibility. I'd fallen in love again in my late thirties, and the reality of being a woman in your late thirties who wants to have another baby is that you're working with a ticking clock. I wasn't ready to get married just yet, but we were getting serious and knew we wanted to be together, so I made a brilliant plan: we'd freeze an embryo and have a baby when we were ready. I spent months stepping away from dinner tables to give myself a shot in the stomach in the bathroom, having wild hormonal changes and retaining water. It felt like months of the worst PMS I'd ever had . . . times a thousand. It felt terrible physically and emotionally, maybe because every medical professional insists on reminding you that after age thirty-five, you're pursuing a *geriatric pregnancy*. Geriatric? Really?? Nobody called John a geriatric father when Cade and Beck were born! Every time my geriatric self went to the doctor, the plan fell apart a little bit more. First, they told me that only one of my ovaries was producing eggs. No big deal! I thought, that's why God gives you two! When it was time to retrieve the eggs, I had seven. It sounded like a lot of eggs to me until I heard them grade my eggs like the chicken eggs in the grocery store. Only two of the seven were Grade A, but hey, that's two chances for a baby! I waited by the phone to hear if any of my geriatric eggs—now embryos—could become a baby. I'll never forget the heartbreaking phone call where a nurse with a gentle voice told me that none of the embryos were viable. There would be no baby for us. It was October, and I knew that the busyness of the next few months would keep me from falling apart. Professionally, the holidays are like the Super Bowl of retail, so I had months of working in our stores and distribution centers, packing up Black (what we at Kendra Scott call Yellow) Friday orders and Christmas presents. Personally, I'm the go-to hostess for every holiday, so at home I had plenty of distraction to keep my mind off the sadness of never welcoming another baby into the world. I created a spooky Halloween, a gorgeous Thanksgiving, and a magical Christmas for our friends and family. I still wasn't feeling great, but I chalked it up to the aftereffects of all those hormones. There was so much uncertainty in the air: I was in love, but not married, and now we would never have a baby. What would the future hold? Would we last? Would we be okay? On New Year's Eve, I made a wish: for a truly happy new year, embracing but on July 4, I was admitted to the emergency room with excruciating pain in my side. I was told that the issue was my gallbladder, and that even though it was bad enough for me to need surgery, the surgery could put me into early labor. I was in the hospital for ten days, and I knew I had to tough it out. I'd been wheeled down to the NICU to see all of the preterm babies and their worried, anguished parents. I'd do whatever it took to keep this baby in as long as I could. That meant eating like a rabbit for the next seven weeks; a diet free of natural or added fats. I ate plain steamed vegetables, steamed chicken, and fruit and vegetable shakes for every meal. As a person who would eat a plate of Mexican food for every meal and never tire of it, this was *definitely* not the plan, but I'd do whatever it took for this baby to arrive healthy.

On August 28, 2013, our little Grey arrived, coloring in the blank spaces in our world that we didn't even know were there. It took thirty hours of labor and a c-section (again, not the plan!) but there he was, my first blue-eyed baby in our family, gazing up at me as though he knew all the secrets of the universe. John drove Cade and Beck to the hospital, and I watched in awe as our two boys met their little brother.

"I love him so much already, Mom," Beck whispered with tears in his eyes as he held him so carefully.

That was not the plan either. I'd been so worried about how Cade and Beck would react to a new baby I hadn't allowed myself to feel hopeful about the relationship. But there it was: love. Not like we planned it, but as it was meant to be. My relationship with Grey's dad didn't work out, but Grey is loved and treasured by both his parents and by a bigger, broader family than the one he was born into, just like I was. I would never call mine or anyone else's household a "broken home," but the fact of a family like ours is that some things *did* break. There is no use in minimizing the pain I felt as a child whose parents would no longer live together in the dream house they'd built with forever in mind. It is not our place as adults to try to invalidate any sorrow our children feel when the families they had shift and change. It *is* sad when things don't work out as we planned them to, and it's okay to mourn for the expectations you had in your life.

Not everyone has a family of origin that makes them feel safe and loved. Not everyone is lucky enough to have had *three* loving parents to support and shape them. As children, there's nothing we can do about the family we're given. You can do all the work in the world and still not be able to force a person to give you the kind of love and support you deserve. How many movies and books do we have about toxic or abusive families, and the pain and harm they cause? As adults, we have the freedom to choose who earns a place in our family, and our friends can become our chosen sisters, brothers, even surrogate parents. I want you to know that this, too, is a family. And choosing to love people regardless of your blood or familial connections is a beautiful, brave thing.

In Japanese pottery, there is a practice called *kintsugi*, where broken pieces of pottery are mended with gold. The result is something more beautiful and unique than what existed before. You can never create identical pieces of *kintsugi* pottery, and the fault lines are where you find the beauty. This is my family, and maybe even yours. Absolutely unique, and totally, completely average.

Fourteen

Own It

If people are hesitant to talk about their relationship failures, they absolutely do not want to discuss their professional failures. I get it, nobody *likes* to fail, even when that "failure" is more like a manageable mistake than an unmitigated disaster. We tell our kids that "everybody makes mistakes," but do we want to be a part of that everybody? No, we want to be the one who gets it all right, all of the time. But the word "professional" does not mean perfect, and my professional life has included plenty of things that some people might call failures, but I call lessons. Dropping out of college was a huge gamble, and when my first business closed, I was now a college dropout with no degree and nothing to show for the years I spent grinding it out trying to convince the world that they should be wearing hats. I closed the doors, I liquidated, and I went back to an office job. *And* I learned so much from that experience that the next time I opened a business I knew exactly what I wasn't going to do, and what worked that I could replicate. I'm not going to convince you in a few pages to undo all of the social conditioning that makes you want to curl up into a ball when you mess up, but I can tell you that I've learned from every one of my mistakes. And because any good teacher knows the difference between showing and telling, I have to share some of *my* favorite "failures" with you.

You're only as good as the people you get advice from.

Let's start with that first lease we signed on South Congress: great location, amazing floor plan, a true game-changer for the business. And . . . one of the biggest mistakes I've made in business. Because I didn't just sign a lease, I signed over a percentage of our profits to the landlord. This was actually a standard lease agreement in Texas at the time, but I signed it without thinking about the future. After all, 6% of nothing is . . . nothing, but 6% of a million dollars is . . . quite a bit of money when you're building a team and still paying yourself less than you've ever made at any job. Sixty thousand dollars could have gone *far* for us. But watching that money flow out of our coffers and up to a landlord *hurt*. It hurt even more when we started doing $3 million a year in business. I was reinvesting every penny we made back into the business, and that 6% would have made a big difference for our growth. The mistake was mine: I'd had a lawyer look over the deal, but I hadn't sought out any insights from other retailers to see if this was a good deal, or if I had any room to negotiate.

I chalk that one up to experience, and the realization that I needed to look far outside of my *own* experience. You're only as good as the people you get advice from, and in the years since I signed that lease, I've surrounded myself with mentors who know what I don't. Many of these people were available to me back then, I just didn't feel confident enough reaching out and asking for their input.

I made plenty of mistakes back in the Hat Box days, but this one has to be the most embarrassing. I thought a custom phone number would make us seem legit to potential customers and look smart on our marketing materials. So, I invested some of my (very) hard-earned cash into a 1-800 number. Potential hat-wearers could dial 1-800-4-HAT-BOX and be connected with . . . me, a friendly voice ready to take their order for any kind of headwear. Smart . . . except that it was one-digit off from an X-rated 1-800 number, and I spent a good portion of my days fielding calls from panting men wondering why I didn't want to describe what I was wearing. I laugh about it now, but I'll tell you what: that would never have happened with our Kendra Scott marketing team.

Your culture is the people, and how your people treat people.

The right people are everything to a business: your culture isn't just your core values, or your product, or what you *say* it is in job interviews or investor meetings. Your culture is the people, and how your people treat people. When we were in our office warehouse space, when going into work felt like stepping into a creative wonderland, I made a huge mistake. She was a gold-plated resume with all the right experience.

Hiring the wrong person is a very expensive mistake, but holding on to the wrong person is even worse.

On paper, she was the right choice. In reality, she was a culture destroyer, not only within our own walls but with our vendors and our buyers. Hiring the wrong person is a very expensive mistake, but holding on to the wrong person is even worse. I hemmed and hawed over letting her go, even as it became clear that the color was being drained from our sunny culture. I spent nights lying awake hoping it would change, that she would change. She didn't. When I sat her down to let her go, she simply said "okay," and left the room. She couldn't possibly have cared less, which tells you how bad of a fit this was for everyone involved. Within twenty-four hours, everyone could feel the light returning to the office. The energy was rebounding with every buyer and vendor call we made to update them about the situation. If she'd stayed, the damage could have been permanent and irreparable. I'd have lost some of the most important people in my life *and* potentially my business, all because I'd chosen a person who didn't represent our values to represent our company. From that moment on, I knew that I'd never again overlook heart and energy in favor of a resume.

One of the MVPs of the Kendra Scott brand is Lon, our very first COO, who joined the team just after we moved into the storefront on South Congress. It was clear that we needed a person with an operational sensibility to take over the details of the business that weren't my strong suit, and I was still gun shy about making another big hire after the last big mistake. So I told everyone I knew—my vendors, my buyers, my friends, my mentors—what I was looking for, and hoped the universe would lead the right person to me. A few weeks later, a friend of mine who worked in banking told me that he had just the guy. Guy? Was he sure this *guy* wanted to work in an office filled with women on a jewelry brand *for* women? He was sure, and five minutes into meeting Lon, I knew he was *our* guy. It wasn't just what he'd done—opened literally hundreds of new stores for Starbucks—but the way he carried himself, with kindness and curiosity and openness. He walked through the store, met with everyone in the office, and we all agreed . . . he was it. To pay him, I cut my pay to below minimum wage and gave him an earned-in-equity position in the company. He'd been offered more money at another company, but this was the best I could do, and he took it. This was all heart, and it was worth it. In five years, we grew our revenue, expanded to over seventy-five stores, and made it possible for me to reinstate my own salary. His partner, John, would come in to help pack orders with my mom in the warehouse—really the office down the hall—and when Lon left us, it was only because he was retiring. By the time he left, we had a dream headquarters and a real warehouse. He focused on his strengths, and I focused on mine, and we had complete faith and trust in each other. He still is family to me and I know either one of us would be there in a second if we needed anything at all. Family at Kendra Scott means forever, not just while you work at the company.

To move on from any mistake or failure, we must be able to own it. When we avoid taking responsibility for our choices, our actions, and what didn't work, shame creeps in and takes root. I once heard that when you point the finger, there are three more pointing back at you. It's freeing to say, *yep, that was me*, not just for yourself but for the people around you. When you're open about your own mistakes, you help create an environment where other people can try . . . and fail. Kids need to see adults apologize when they're wrong, and explain what they could have done differently. So do adults! I would rather have an employee make a decision—even if it's different from one I would make— than sit there and do nothing. Even at the store level, we give every associate the power to please a customer. They don't need manager approval to offer a discount or take a return, they can just do it. If it turns out to be a mistake, we can always talk it out. There's so much to learn from what we do "wrong," and at least trying creates an opportunity for progress.

The pandemic created an environment where everyone in business was suddenly an amateur. Even the most seasoned executives—those who had weathered the 2008 crash and other disasters—had never navigated a global pandemic. As executives at Kendra Scott, we had to be honest about this: that we didn't know exactly what to do, but we were going to try things, a *lot* of things, and see what worked. To survive, we needed our employees to do the same: to take a risk, to throw out their big ideas even if they seemed silly. If they didn't work, okay! Onto the next one! We tried same-day delivery with a fleet of cars, thinking we'd be as good as Amazon. Nope! Turns out, curbside pickup was just fine, and investing in a bunch of yellow-wrapped vehicles was not the game-changer we hoped. We created a virtual styling system that people *loved*, and we adapted the Kendra Gives Back events—a staple of our store experience—to be virtual. Both of these are elements of the business that are sticking around even as the world opens back up. When we pretend to be perfect, we make it impossible for those around us to be imperfect, and people *are* imperfect. It's what makes us interesting and creative and alive. Owning it doesn't mean you beat yourself up and replay your mistakes in your head forever. You can own it, learn from it, and move forward.

When you're no longer ashamed of what didn't work, you can actually start to see it with clearer eyes. I can see today that the Hat Box was a gift to me. A painful, expensive gift, but still cheaper than college and an MBA. As insecure as I was in *many* rooms for my lack of formal business education, I had what a lot of people didn't: real-life experience building a business. When you're faced with a failure of any kind, you have two choices: quit or try again. Look, after every divorce I told myself, "Never again! I'll live alone for the rest of my days, no more love for me!" And then I tried again. I failed again. And I tried . . . again. Because life, when you think about it, is really, really short. We are just a blink in the great stretch of time, and I don't believe that we were put on this earth to be perfect, but to learn and to grow.

What we tell children is true: everyone does make mistakes. My own could fill many, many books, but like most mistakes, they're not all that interesting: I run late, I miss things, I forget my manners or (rarely) a birthday. What happened matters, but not as much as the changes that come afterward. I make mistakes all the time, and then I own them, even if what I'm owning is that I stayed too late at the office and that the boys' favorite roast beef dinner is going to be replaced with Chinese take-out. Because the only real failure in life and in business is refusing to look at your mistakes and missteps. Hold them up to the light, own them, and then put them down. Let them become the stepping-stones between where you've been and where you're going, a path for other people to follow.

Hitting the Floor

The best place to cry is always on the ground; the space beside your bed, where nobody will see you if they open the door, the bathroom, where the tile will cool your red cheeks. You need the sureness of the earth below you, even if it's threatening to swallow you whole. I've cried like this a few times in my life: when Rob died, during my divorce(s), and when I was eleven years old.

My dad's parents—Grandpa Dick and Grandma Irene—were like a second set of parents to me, especially after my mom and dad divorced. Some kids might have complained about "having" to go to their grandparents' house, but I *loved* it. My cousin Kelly and I were their little princesses; Grandma loved to have us out in her rose garden, and Grandpa loved an audience while he tinkered in the garage. He drove a Chevy Impala, a great big whale of a car that I'd watch for through the picture window of our living room on our special Grandpa/Granddaughter dates. When I heard the rumble of the engine, I'd race out the front door and into the front door of his car, sliding across the bench seat to sit right next to him. This was the eighties, so there were no booster seats and nobody thought to put kids in the backseat. Instead, at sudden stops your mom (or Grandpa, in this case) would shoot their arm out across your chest like a human seat belt, thinking there was no form of protection more sufficient than a human forearm. I'll admit I still do this decades later to my own kids, who are absolutely bewildered by the instinct. Grandpa was one of my favorite people on Earth: he wore cozy cardigan sweaters and smelled like laundry detergent and Irish Spring soap, the greatest men's fragrance I've ever smelled. We'd drive around Kenosha, visiting his friends at the fire department or stopping for ice cream, and he'd tell me stories about his childhood. I was the happiest girl in the world in the front seat of that Impala.

Grandpa's Happy Place was the garage. Sometimes he'd be working on the car, and sometimes he'd be turning an empty Coke can into a little sculpture or tinkering with something he *knew* he could fix. It was June 4, that magical last week of school where you can *feel* summer just around the corner, where kids are cleaning out their desks and getting ready to say goodbye to the school year and teachers are planning class parties. So obviously, I needed some Lee press-on nails in gold to make sure I made a splash at the end of fifth grade. My dad—ever patient, and somehow understanding that these press-on nails were an actual fashion emergency—picked me up from school as usual and agreed to make a pit stop at the mall so I could get the exact nails I wanted. I buzzed in and out of that mall like a girl on a mission, ready to get to Grandma and Grandpa's house, pour myself a pop and do my nails. Grandpa would get a kick out of this, I knew. He'd laugh and ask how I'd get any work done "with talons like that" and tell me I was beautiful. Grandma was in Milwaukee taking care of Kelly while Jo Ann was at a fashion show in Paris, so it would be just me and Grandpa, which meant he would probably make me chicken and rice Campbell's soup and buttered toast and applesauce on the side. I'm telling you, this was the *life*.

Dad dropped me off outside with a kiss, and I walked in the front door, dropped my bags in the kitchen, and called out for him. Grandpa *loved* playing tricks on me, so I peeked around the corner into the living room and entryway, expecting him to jump out and scare me. The coast was clear, so I stepped into the cool, dark garage. The radio was playing Grandpa's favorite station—boring talk radio—and I could see him under my aunt's car, probably waiting to slide out and scare me as soon as I got close. "Hey, Grandpa!" I said again, stepping closer. No response.

"Graaaaaandpa!" I called in a teasing voice, expecting him to grab my ankle and scare the daylights out of me. Nothing.

When I bent down to tell him he wasn't going to get me this time, his face was blue and all I could hear was the sound of my own voice screaming, "Grandpa! Grandpa! Grandpa!"

I've been told I ran next door to get the neighbors, but I don't remember that. I just remember sitting on the front steps, shaking, asking all of the adults around me if my grandfather was alive. The question was answered by the paramedics rolling his body out of the garage, covered in a sheet.

I threw those press-on nails in the garbage like they were evidence of my crime. I'd had to go to the mall instead of right to Grandpa. I could have done something. This was my fault, and I knew it.

Mental health care was simply not a part of the conversation in 1980s Kenosha, Wisconsin. I'd undergone a seriously traumatic event, and I couldn't think, couldn't sleep, couldn't speak. I couldn't bear to look at my own parents, in fear that they'd know exactly what I was thinking: it's my fault. I needed to isolate myself from my family, so my godparents, who lived next door to us, took me in. I spent my days laying on the floor of their guest bedroom, letting my tears soak the carpet, trying to rewrite the ending of this story, trying to undo the wrong I'd done. I didn't want to go to the funeral— everyone would see me and know how guilty I was—but agreed at the last minute to attend with my godparents. In the casket, Grandpa didn't look blue anymore, but he didn't look like Grandpa either. He was a wax figurine wearing my Grandpa's clothes. He didn't smell like Irish Spring or laundry detergent. I took a letter from my pocket and slipped it into the casket beside him.

I love you, Grandpa.
I'm so, so sorry.
Please forgive me.
I love you.
Kendra

Death seemed to lurk around every corner, threatening to take everyone from me. Was my mom okay in Chicago? What would happen to my grandmother without the man she'd been in love with since she was eighteen? If my dad was five minutes late to pick me up—rare for a man of his word, but it did happen—I was sure he'd died in a car accident. Every few weeks, my father took me to visit Grandpa at the cemetery. Dad would sweep the grass from the headstone and place fresh flowers beside it. I would lay on top of the grass and talk to him. When Dad wasn't looking, I'd bury a letter in the ground, hoping it would get to him.

Losing the people you love does not get easier; there is no grief muscle you can build up to make yourself strong enough not to crumble when the people you love die. Grandpa's death wasn't practice for losing Rob; it was a whole different kind of loss. And then . . . there was Holley.

Holley and I met at age twenty-two, an era of acrylic French manicures, tanning beds, and big, blonde hair. The men we were dating—men we considered sophisticated because they were thirty years old—were best friends and had introduced us on a double date. We were like tan, blonde magnets: instantly connected, and for life. Holley and I were never a part of the other's friend groups because we wanted each other all to ourselves: doing each other's makeup before nights out dancing until the DJ turned the house lights back on, holding each other's hair back after a little too much fun, and in a move that Holley would claim was the impetus for my jewelry business, Holley pulling one of my earrings out of my own puke. I know, but that's friendship, isn't it? Holley had a contagious love for life, she was a ball of energy and light whenever she stepped in the room. Those men who introduced us left our lives and became footnotes in the story, but we were the main characters.

Holley was there for the Hat Box, even though her head was too big for me to outfit her properly (7⅝ if you need to know, that's a big melon!). She was one of the first friends who wore my jewelry and hyped it up to the moms in her playgroups and on the very early 00s reality TV show she had with her husband. In life, we have many soul mates, and Holley was one of mine. We talked about life the way married people do: how we'd retire and have cabins on the same land, or travel the world together.

And then, cancer showed up.

Holley's youngest was still nursing, and she figured that the pain in her breast must be a clogged duct. But the clog didn't seem to go away, and when the baby moved on to solid foods and Holley finally told the doctor about it, it was already bad. The chemo took her hair, her eyelashes, her strength, but not her fire: when her hair grew back like the down of a duckling, she dyed it hot pink. Every time I rubbed her back as she vomited from the chemo, she reminded me of the times she'd done the same for me after a few too many shots of tequila. And every time she had to go to the hospital for chemo infusions, I brought her a new piece of jewelry to lift her spirits and doll her up. She opened every box with joy and gratitude and sent me photos from the infusion center. These little gifts were big for her: a reminder that those of us on the outside were thinking of her and loving her, even when we needed to keep our distance for the sake of her immune system. For a year, we walked a tightrope over the unthinkable: that Holley could die, could leave behind her beautiful children. I'd seen up close how Katie had suffered in the wake of her mother's death, and I couldn't bear to think of Holley's children going to bed without a tuck-in from their mother or blowing out birthday candles without her singing to them. I left every visit with her trying to soak her up like a sponge, memorizing the way she laughed, the crinkles at the corner of her eyes, her favorite nail polish color. When she turned forty, we celebrated like she'd won the Super Bowl, and when she had her last infusion and was declared cancer free, we celebrated like she'd won two Super Bowls. Holley had always been a person who loved life, but nearly losing hers had given her an even greater appreciation for what she had. When her hair grew back in and she dyed it hot pink, she led every fundraiser she could for breast cancer research.

But she was never really cancer free, and it didn't take long for her doctor to tell her that the cancer had turned metastatic, setting up grade 4 tumors in her spine and her bones. This was a worst-case scenario: there is no cure for metastatic breast cancer, which means that the treatment—if it works—never ends. You have metastatic breast cancer for the rest of your abbreviated life.

The stages of grief were introduced by Elisabeth Kübler-Ross to describe the phases a dying person goes through: Denial, Anger, Bargaining, Depression, Acceptance. I have weaved in and out of these and plenty of other stages in my life, but I saw Holley step quickly into defiance: she was aware of the statistics and the reality of the situation, and her anger fueled her to make a difference for other women.

Crying on her couch, we raged about how many women go undiagnosed, how many funerals are held every year for women whose cancer just wasn't caught in time or had spread undetected. She hadn't even thought about metastasis that first year—should she have?

There's a viral video that Holley made on YouTube after she was diagnosed with metastatic cancer. In it, she's staring down into her camera while Rachel Platten's "Fight Song" plays, holding up index cards that tell her story, but also the bigger story: that 6-10% are diagnosed as metastatic initially and 30% are re-diagnosed as metastatic, and that 40,000 people are lost each year to metastatic breast cancer. I watched this at my desk at work after she posted it to Facebook, chills running down my body. When she holds up the cards that say "There is no cure" and "My treatment will never . . . ever . . . ever . . . ever . . . ever be done. Until my journey on earth is over," she takes a deep breath and shakes her head into the camera. And she keeps going. "Statistics say . . . upon re-diagnosis I had only 26 months to live." I know from the way her nose twitches at this card that this statistic is a punch in the gut to her, but she's not done with her message. Nobody, she points out, wants to talk about metastatic cancer. It's frightening, and we don't like to be frightened. We were, though—Holley's friends, her family— we were frightened of a world without her.

We watched that video gain hundreds, then thousands, then over a million views on Facebook. She was invited onto *Good Morning America*, where she met Rachel Platten on video conference and spread her message across America. We watched her acceptance, her dedication, her bravery touch lives across the world, reaching people she'd never have the chance to meet in real life. She was not a number, or a statistic, and neither were the people leaving comments about their own experiences with metastatic breast cancer.

Call it magical thinking, but I really thought Holley was going to make it. Even when the experimental drug she was on stopped working and I stayed up all night calling researchers in Germany trying to get her into a new clinical trial. Even when she went to the hospital for pneumonia. Even when she entered hospice, the idea that a woman so full of life was facing the end of hers felt impossible. She was Holley. She was a mother.

Holley taught me that words aren't everything. In her video, she holds up a card that says "Sometimes it's okay to say nothing." She and her MBC friends—the #lifers, they called themselves—had made a (partial) list of the things they were tired of hearing. Things like "but you're so young!" or "you must not have taken care of yourself" (I'm not a violent person, but if I ever heard someone say that to Holley or any other cancer patient I'm not sure I wouldn't slap them). There are moments when words aren't necessary, or when they're completely insufficient. I could never summarize for Holley what her friendship meant to me, the way she'd become an indelible part of my being. And as it became obvious that her time was running out, the being was far more important than the saying.

We spent the last night of Holley's life making scrapbooks and writing letters for her kids. She was weak and tired, and her beautiful hands shook, but she wanted something to help them remember. I didn't know this was the last night of Holley's life, I just knew that I wanted every moment I could have with her. Nearly twenty years of friendship meant that our time together had ebbed and flowed; businesses and children and life had taken us closer and further apart. I wished I'd flowed more toward her, but here I was: brushing her teeth, washing her body, giving her all the love I had, while I could. I kissed her goodbye at 9:30 pm.

"I'll be back in the morning to finish our project. I love you, my little duck." I kissed the top of her fuzzy head, and she smiled.

"Love you, Kendra," she whispered, her eyes closing.

The next time I saw her was in the funeral home. Grandpa hadn't looked like Grandpa, but this was *not* Holley. It couldn't be. She was cold and stiff, and her coloring was all wrong. We'd done each other's makeup a thousand times over the years, and I knew her beauty routine like I knew my own. But this was not the same as getting dolled up for a night out, not even close. This was the last time I could touch her, talk to her, *be* with her, and it wasn't her. I swept eyeshadow onto her lids and blended blush and bronzer into her cheeks. I lined and filled in her lips, and I could hear her joking: *You better pick a good color, Kendra. I want to look good in the afterlife.* I let my tears and my laughter exist together in this holy and horrible moment. I filled in her brows and swiped on mascara. I put on the hot pink necklace I'd given her after one of those many chemo infusions. It was bold and bright like her personality, and she'd worn it like armor to everything from treatments to speaking events. I kissed her goodbye, and went upstairs for the visitation.

And then, I hit the floor again. When the shock of the loss and the tasks of the funeral were over, all that was left was the pain. I wasn't a little girl anymore—I didn't think this was my fault—but the trauma of this loss rang that same bell inside of me. There had to be something I could do. I'm a fixer: present me with a problem and I'll find ten new ways to solve it, and twenty more if the first ten don't work out. But not everything in life can be solved. There was nothing I could do to save my grandfather, or to save Holley or Rob. I had done everything I could do: I had shown up, had loved them, had shared deep relationships. And that's what we do: we show up, and we keep showing up when things are hard, or exhausting, or downright terrible. We cannot fix it all for everyone, but we can do our best to ease the burden for those around us.

Holley—like Rob and my grandfather—is an angel on my shoulder, a voice in the back of my head. I got up off that bathroom floor because I'd seen Holley do it at least a hundred times—literally, every time chemo knocked her on her ass, and a few times when we'd been a bit overserved in our wild twenties. I got up off that bathroom floor because I watched my mom do it after she lost the love of her life.

There's a sixth stage of grief, introduced by David Kessler, who worked with Elisabeth Kübler-Ross on their book *On Death and Dying*. The stage is Finding Meaning, the drive we all have to create something meaningful out of our despair. He writes, "Loss is simply what happens to you in life. Meaning is what you make happen." Holley made meaning through her activism and her mothering, through her relationships and the way she lives on in each of the people who loved her. Holley knew that her time was limited, and that the fight to save her own life was never just about her own life, but about the lives of those millions of people who saw her video, and the many more who wouldn't see it but would live that same reality. To me, that's the crux of finding meaning: moving beyond your own experience and into the way your experience connects you to the world.

Holley is why our buy one, gift one program exists; with any purchase of a specific collection during the month of October, a piece of jewelry is gifted to a woman battling cancer, a tangible way we could make life just a little more beautiful for someone. She's why we support Inheritance of Hope, which provides counseling and support to families with a parent with a terminal illness. We sponsor trips to Disney for families with a parent diagnosed with terminal metastatic breast cancer. That Inheritance of Hope trip was one of Holley's favorite moments with her family, and the things that matter to her will always matter to me. I have 0% chance of curing cancer without a college degree, like I had 0% chance of saving my grandfather from the heart attack that took his life. But what I can do as a business owner is *give* without counting the cost, without an agenda, with the goal of making a woman feel a spark of joy in the face of illness. Funding research with the Breast Cancer Research Fund won't bring back Holley, or Katie's mom. But someday, it will save *someone's* mother, someone's sister, someone's Holley. Jewelry is a talisman. For ages, it's been a symbol of status or power or intention. For these kiddos and their families, it's a talisman of hope, of something they can hold and remember. Something to imbue with power and meaning.

In every obituary and on every headstone, it lists a person's birth and death years, separated by a dash. One of Holley's greatest lessons to me was to "live the dash," however long or short it may be. Most of us have no idea when our lives will be over, but Holley knew her life would be shorter than she'd expected, and she lived the hell out of that dash. She poured herself into her relationships and her children, she loved fiercely, and left us all knowing that we mattered deeply to her. The best way I know to honor her life is to make sure that I spend *my* dash wisely. I want to make sure that the years I have are filled to the brim with *life*: with joy and laughter, and the kind of pain and sorrow that means I loved people as well as I could. There are plenty of times in life where you'll hit the floor, and it's okay to stay there for a minute, or even a day. You're not alone. Other people have been there, and other people are experiencing that same pain, maybe even in this same moment. You'll get up again, even if you need help. Depression, grief, and mental health are real and if you can't pick yourself up, there is no shame in needing someone else to pull you up and help you stay on your feet.

I've watched Holley's video countless times since she died, and I will never hear "Fight Song" without tears pricking my eyes. The meaning we've made is not just a reflection on the fact of her illness and her death, but the truth of her *life*: she had the best laugh, the worst eighties hair you've ever seen, an incredible work ethic, and she made a great brownie. She spoke volumes with the raising of an eyebrow, she hated "Mom Hair" but she *loved* being a mom. She was here. She mattered. And the fight goes on.

How to Fight

Speaking of fighting, you should know that I'm not much of a fighter, at least not physically. Metaphorically, I know how to get up when I'm knocked down, but I'll never throw the first punch. And everything I know about fighting I learned in a Pizza Hut parking lot in small-town Wisconsin.

There's really never anything for middle school kids to do, no matter where you live, but our options in Kenosha were pretty limited: you could hang out at the skate shop, the mall in Racine, and in the summer months, the lake. And if you had the cash, you could go to Pizza Hut for dinner. For younger readers, Pizza Hut used to be a place, not just an app or a small storefront in a strip mall. Pizza Hut was the place, actually: a sit-down restaurant with giant, pebbled plastic glasses filled to the brim with Coke served by the pitcher, a salad bar for the fancier guests, and low-hanging stained-glass lamps above the tables. For a middle schooler, there's not much else you're looking for as far as ambiance.

Katie was one of the only close friends I had aside from my dad at this point, and he had more of a social life than I did. Katie was always a tough kid, but her mom's death had made her *tough* tough: she wore heavy black eyeliner and had a real "try me" attitude, and though the two of us looked like an odd couple, we were perfectly matched. Katie was in a house of boys: her dad and her three brothers. I was living mostly with my dad in our little condo. We may have been outsiders, but together we never felt like we were outside of anything. After the seventh grade dance, Katie and I walked to Pizza Hut and then we were going to go back to my dad's house for a sleepover. We sat down and ordered deep-dish pizza and unlimited pop. We were feeling very grown-up—we were at a restaurant! Alone!—and then we saw them. Every group of Mean Girls has a ringleader, a Regina George who leads the pack and selects the victims. We'll call ours Brittany. Grown-ups know that hurt people hurt people, that every bully has a backstory that usually involves their own emotional or physical abuse. But kids don't know that, just like they don't know that someone else's behavior toward you says more about *them* than it does about you. I wasn't Brittany's only target, but it felt like I was her favorite one. I'd given up on trying to win her over, and my strategy was to just avoid her, pretend she didn't exist. You can guess how well that worked.

As soon as the hostess had seated us and promised us a pitcher of Coke, we could hear Brittany and her posse trying to get our attention, shouting our names, throwing balled-up napkins our way when the servers weren't looking.

"Ignore them," Katie said, a fake smile plastered on her face. I gave her a big, fake laugh like she'd told a great joke, and we *did* ignore them. They'd already been served by the time we'd been seated, and it *was* Friday night, so eventually the server would need that table turned over. They couldn't stay here all night, could they? They could, sort of. They wandered out to the parking lot, and I tried to keep myself from looking through the window to see where they'd congregated.

Once Katie and I had worked our way through our cheese pizza, a girl named Jenn appeared, snapping her gum next to our table.

"Kendra," she said in a singsong voice, "Brittany wants to fight you."

Fight me? *Fight me?* My mind went blank. Katie's hands were already balled into fists, and I heard myself say, "I'm a lady, and ladies don't fight. If Brittany would like to talk with me, I'd be more than happy to have a discussion, but I won't be fighting anybody."

Jenn laughed as if I'd told her a joke and walked back outside, returning all of thirty seconds later to lean over the table like an angry school principal.

"Brittany would *love* to talk, Kendra. Come on out whenever you're ready."

Her tone was far from sincere, and now I was sweating, shaking, and looking for the emergency exits. I wasn't going to fight anyone! I had just done my nails, and the closest I'd been to a physical altercation was a doorbusters sale at Kohl's. Surely, I thought, their parents would pick them up soon.

Katie and I waited as long as humanly possible to pay our check, and then we stepped outside into the cold Wisconsin air, and into a circle of my classmates, with Brittany at the center. I took a deep breath, preparing to speak my piece, and Brittany immediately stepped forward . . . and sucker-punched me in the chin. My head rang like in the cartoons, and I hit the concrete, my bones rattling. I heard cheering, laughter, and then the pain arrived, not just in my head but all over my body. Brittany was on top of me, raining punches on my head, my face. All around me were the feet and legs of the kids who watched as Brittany ripped my art from the hallway walls or shouted "Stickster!" at me across the cafeteria, cheering like they were watching Hulk Hogan and Mr. Wonderful. I was screaming, crying, trying to protect my face while Brittany used me as a punching bag.

I heard him before I saw him. My dad's souped-up Toyota Supra came tearing into the parking lot, tires squealing. All 6'3" of Wisconsin Cowboy Lawyer got out of that car, and the kids scattered like roaches. Katie, who'd run inside to call my dad from the pay phone, rushed to my side. Brittany didn't stop her assault until my dad strode across the pavement and picked her up by her collar. In my memory, she dangles in the air, swinging her fists and kicking, the kids shouting, "Put her down! Put her down!"

"Don't. You. Ever. Touch. My. Daughter!" he shouted, his voice rising with every word until it was a roar echoing across the dark sky. He was shaking with anger, but in his eyes I saw his heart breaking. Since middle school started, I'd been miserable.

"Dad," I begged almost every day, "I need to switch schools. Please, please, please, don't make me go back."

"Kill 'em with kindness, Kendra," he'd reply, kissing me on the cheek before sending me off to school. Dad was adamant that nobody could push me out of *my* school, that I could outlast any of these kids.

But that night changed something. I'd seen my dad mad before, but not like this. He paced around the living room shouting like he was giving closing arguments in the trial of his life, talking about how he was going to give the parents—no, the school—no, the school board—a piece of his mind. Dad held bags of frozen peas to my swollen face until they were soft, and I cried not just from the physical pain, but from the psychological torture I'd been through since middle school started. It wasn't enough to humiliate me. Brittany had to degrade me, dehumanize me, literally beat me down. And why? I'd been nice, and when that hadn't worked, I'd ignored her. The only other thing to do was give up.

I rarely saw my dad cry, but tonight his face was wet when he tucked me in.

"Dad," I cried, "please just let me switch schools."

"Sure, baby," he said in that croaky voice you get when you're trying not to cry. "Whatever you need."

I fell asleep in his bed that night, and spent my entire weekend at home, too embarrassed to do anything. But on Sunday night, I did what I always did: I laid out my outfit for the next day, finished my homework, and made my lunch. On Monday morning, my dad and I got in the Supra and drove to school, me with a fat lip and him in his smart suit and cowboy boots.

"Are you sure?" he asked me as we pulled into the parking lot, and I nodded.

"Let's kill 'em with kindness," I smiled, and we walked into my middle school together.

I'm sure that Brittany went home on Friday night thinking she'd won the fight, but she didn't. I'm also sure that she
spent the entire weekend willing her home phone not to ring,
but it did, and she got a whopping three days of out of school
suspension for her parking lot assault. It was a sentence my
father had quietly argued for while I hid out in my room,
bringing all of his courtroom bravado to the principal's office.
Brittany wasn't there on Monday morning, but my dad still
walked me to my locker, kissed me goodbye, and let his heavy
boots do the talking as he walked down the long corridor
and into the bright light of a Wisconsin morning. Brittany
and I never became good friends, but she never touched me
again. I went through the rest of middle school in relative
peace; if our teachers forced us into a group project, I'd be
friendly and kind, but I would *never* seek out her approval.

What does the least popular girl in school do when she's
been beaten down in a Pizza Hut parking lot and still has a
haircut that makes her grandmother's friends think she's a
boy? She does the only thing she *can* do: she decides to run
for Student Council president.

This is the first concrete memory I have of knowing my
purpose in life. It wasn't about the destination (in this case, a
folding table in the teacher's lounge where the Student Council held their monthly meetings), it was about what it represented. I'd put up new posters every time these girls ripped
them down. I'd make sure that no kid had to eat alone in the
bathroom. I would be made fun of and mocked, but I
wouldn't let *anyone* keep me down. Was I delusional? Maybe
a little bit. But I was a stick-thin middle schooler with a mush-
room perm and a rat tail, so what did I have to lose? I spent

my nights with poster board and colored paper spread across every inch of my bedroom. My dad sat right next to me, using up packs of scented magic markers and bottles of glitter until I was confident I had enough campaign materials screaming my slogan: Kendra Can!

In movies about middle school or high school, the nerd who thinks they can be student body president is ridiculed and mocked. Well, that's what happened in real life, too. My beautiful bubble-letter posters were scribbled on or torn down, and every evening I made more. On election day, I put on my best leg warmers and my favorite Guess sweatshirt and walked into school with my permed head held high. I promised myself that if I lost, I wouldn't cry. I wouldn't eat in the bathroom. And I didn't.

Because I won the election. I wasn't Stickster anymore, I was *President Stickster*. Brittany, by the way, was secretary. She took notes during the meetings I ran.

Brittany was good practice for a lifetime of being who I am, and doing what I love, a lesson in knowing that some people *just don't get it*. That's their problem, not yours. The urge to defend ourselves against hateful people is strong and primal; we want people to like us, to see us as good. We're built for connection, and to be faced with people who intentionally do not want to connect with you? It *hurts*. That's okay. Let it hurt.

But do not let someone else's opinion of you become *your* opinion of you. Long past middle school, it's easy to origami ourselves into another person's idea of us. If I'd just worn some Izod polo shirts and joined the tennis team, if I'd just conformed to what Brittany and her crowd deemed "cool"—I'd have gained some short-lived friendships and some cheap social capital. But I'd have lost so much more. I'd have become the people who tormented me, and even if they deserved some form of retribution, I didn't want to be the one to do it.

In the decades since that night in the Pizza Hut parking lot, I've been invited to plenty of fights and politely declined. This doesn't make me a pushover or a victim, it has helped me retain my power. A person who is invested in you and the relationship you have will want you to know when you've messed up and what you can improve upon, and they'll bring that feedback to you respectfully and in a spirit of kindness. But sometimes, a person's problem with you is just that: *their problem*. A cutting remark, a betrayal of your trust . . . these aren't examples of constructive criticism within the context of a healthy relationship, they're invitations to a fight that you don't have to attend. There's a saying that goes "you can't make sense out of nonsense." You can't. Brittany's hatred of me was nonsense—more about whatever was happening in her own life than who I was as an awkward tween.

---

*I do believe that women have a sacred
responsibility to support one another . . .
and that we are also allowed healthy
conflict among each other. But we
need to make sure the fight counts for
something, that it matters.*

I've stepped away from fights, and I've stepped into some, too. Because the thing about bullies is that they never really go away, and this stuff we call "middle school drama" easily carries on into our adulthood. The scenery changes, and the stakes just get higher. I do believe that women have a sacred responsibility to support one another . . . and that we are also allowed healthy conflict among each other. But we need to make sure the fight *counts* for something, that it matters. At a soccer game years ago, I was seated with a pack of mostly moms, doing what moms do: chatting and trying to cheer at the right time. One of our boys' teammates had a stay-at-home dad, a guy who had dedicated his life to the same thing a lot of these moms had: the very real, very intense job of running a family's day-to-day life. His wife was a renowned doctor, doing the very real, very intense job of saving lives. I don't know when the conversation turned to Dr. Mom, but when it did, I was shocked.

"He does *everything*," one mom snipped. "She doesn't even come to the games."

I looked around—this dad was one of the only dads there at a 5:00 pm game *for either team*—were they serious? Another mom piped up, "I know, it's so *sad*."

Oh, hell no.

"Oh, are you talking about Dr. Mom?" I said, pretending like I hadn't heard anything else. "Isn't it great that she's out there saving lives and her husband is here to do his part? I love it. You know, she just won a huge award for her work *saving lives*. I think it's so great that they work together like this. It's just *great*." I laid it on thick, with my biggest smile, and boom! The conversation shifted. Does this always work?

Of course not! I spent years trying to win over a woman in my social circle who would literally turn to give me the cold shoulder in public. One night, in a call-back to that Pizza Hut parking lot, she confronted me at a party to ask me to "step outside." I stepped outside half-expecting a repeat of the Brittany situation, but instead she just stood there coldly while I begged her to tell me what was *wrong*, what I could possibly do to make our relationship this bad. She sputtered, flabbergasted, and finally just said, "Look at you." And I *did* look at me. I was standing outside in the cold, wasting a great outfit and a great party to beg for the approval of a person who just . . . didn't like me. I went back inside and moved on with my life.

We do not all need to be friends, but for the love of all that is good and holy we need to make sure that the conflicts we're choosing are worth it, and that we speak respectfully to and about each other.

We do *not* all need to be friends, but for the love of all that is good and holy we need to make sure that the conflicts we're choosing are worth it, and that we speak respectfully to and about each other. All of these anti-bullying campaigns focus on children, but who do children learn from? Us. And when they hear us ripping another woman to shreds for the way she dresses or how much she works or for staying at home with her kids . . . they learn that it's okay to disrespect and disparage anyone who is different from them. I'm not saying I've never gossiped, but I do know that it's never once made me actually feel better about myself, and when I hear people do it around *me*, I instantly wonder if they do it *about* me.

It's rare that someone will actually *want* to say it to your face, and when they do, you have the right and the responsibility to stand up for yourself, too. Here's an example: One summer night I was standing in the front yard of my big, beautiful home that I built and paid for myself (well, I paid for it to be built myself, I wasn't swinging any hammers), throwing a tennis ball for my giant English sheepdog, Duke. I was still new to the neighborhood, and I hadn't met my neighbors, but somewhere between the tenth and the hundredth tennis ball toss, I heard their back door open and a group of people spill out onto their patio. I swear to you I wasn't eavesdropping, but I heard my own name float over the wall between our homes almost instantly.

"Yeah, Kendra Scott. The jewelry lady. Her ex-husband built the house for her. Pretty nice, huh?" It was a man speaking, and the other voices joining in were also men, chiming in in agreement that they'd heard the same thing, that the secret to my success was my ex-husband.

My ex-husband did not build this house for me, or write me a check to build it, and I felt my cheeks burn with anger and embarrassment. *Is this what people think of me? That I'm just a housewife with a hobby?* My brain started calculating all the clever things I could say if I scaled the wall and jumped into the middle of their dinner party: *Actually, I was just inducted into the Texas Business Hall of Fame,* or *Actually, my company was just valued at a billion-dollar valuation,* or *I was one of only twenty women in the U.S. to carry the title of a self-made billionaire.* I threw the ball for Duke one last time, and the neighbors' conversation moved on. But I did not. I yelled right through the trees that fenced our properties, "Hi! It's Kendra. Sounds like you all are having some fun!" Immediately there was the silence that tends to fall when a group of people realize the subject of their gossip has overheard them. A voice came back over, awkwardly. "Oh, hi, Kendra, you should come and join us . . ." This was clearly not really an invite, I could tell from the crack in his voice. But I went to my kitchen, grabbed a bottle of wine, leashed up Duke, and marched over to my neighbor's house, where I let myself in the front door and walked out onto the deck and into the dinner party where I'd just been the topic of conversation. I plopped the bottle of Domaines Ott rosé onto the outdoor dining table and introduced myself.

"I'm Kendra," I said. "I should have come over to introduce myself sooner, because I'm your next-door neighbor. Our houses are so close together that I happened to overhear your conversation." Duke panted happily next to me—didn't he know it was time to look intimidating? My neighbor turned white as a sheet, and then red. "So," I continued, handing him the bottle of wine, "I just want to clear up any confusion. I built my house myself, with my own money." I said it kindly and sincerely, with a smile on my face pulling up a chair. "Any questions? Anyone? I'm right here, so ask away!"

Was it awkward? For him, I guess, because the next day his wife sent me flowers and a card apologizing for her husband. We do *not* need to apologize for our husbands, they can and should do that themselves, but I appreciated the gesture.

Power—real power—isn't something that you wield like a weapon, it's something that you protect.

There are plenty of people who would hold that grudge forever, who would have started a passive-aggressive war via Christmas lights or by letting their dogs poop on each other's front yards or walked up to that front door looking for a fight. But power—real power—isn't something that you wield like a weapon, it's something that you protect. Those neighbors are some of my favorite people now, and we all laugh about that evening. When we fly off the handle, lose our cool, or obsess over how *wrong* someone else is, we're squandering our power. Now, I've worked really hard for what I have and where I am, but I don't fight *people*. I fight ideas and complacency and systems. My grandfather used to tell me that when you wrestle a pig, you both get dirty . . . but the pig likes it.

When I walked into that middle school with a fat lip, I did it proudly (and yes, awkwardly). Maybe my dad just thought he was walking me into school, but he was giving me a template for how to walk through this world. Because as we grow up, not all of us grow out of middle school. Some bullies just get bigger and smarter and meaner, and you can spend your life trying to get even or keep your eyes on your own paper and move forward as who you really are. Life will bring you plenty of fights: for what you believe in, for who you are, for what you want. The past few years have given us plenty to fight for and about, but you get to decide what's worth fighting for and what's worth walking away from. Not every comment needs a reply, not every push deserves a shove, and the more time we waste on the fight with each other . . . the less time we have to build together.

Seventeen

The Power of No

"No" is one of the scariest words in the English language. Or so I've been told. Personally, I *love* a *no*. I come alive when I hear this word, as though I've been given a surprise gift. Tell me I can't do something and I'm fired up and ready to prove you wrong. *No* is a huge motivator for me, but I get why it's frightening to so many people: it can feel like a rejection, like a failure, like proof that whatever our Big Idea is—even if it's really just a little idea—it's no good. Turn that *no* around and what do you get? *On*. That idea doesn't apply to personal boundaries—as I've explained to my teenage sons—but for so many situations, it's an invitation to think creatively about how to make our dreams happen. There's a popular phrase that's used in sales trainings and motivational speaking events: *the worst they can say is no.* Having trained hundreds of employees and coached dozens of friends, I would never say that because it's not true.

Once I finally had that rep in Dallas, I had the opportunity to attend my very first market: a multiday event where buyers from small boutiques and major stores toured showrooms to place their orders for the coming season. I already had a great presence in Austin boutiques, but I'd set a goal to get my designs in Harold's, a high-end department store with locations across Texas. Typically, reps do what their title implies: they *represent* their clients to buyers. But I knew that nobody could sell me like I could sell me, and I walked into the market with my tea box, my (upgraded) business cards, and my goal at the front of my mind, and found that buyer. After ten minutes—it felt like hours—she handed me her card and told me to send some samples to her office because she'd *love* to consider them for the catalog. I was in heaven. I was still small and relatively new to the industry; I'd set a lofty goal and it felt like I was going to achieve it. My rep told me—gently—that I'd be wasting my time and money sending samples to Harold's. The buyer would get hundreds of boxes after this event, and my designs would be lucky to be opened by an assistant's assistant. I thanked her genuinely for her insight, and felt the pilot light of ambition spark to life inside of me.

Back at home, I did what I'd watched my mother do a million times back in her Mary Kay HQ at our house in Kenosha: I wrapped the samples up in tissue paper, sprayed them with a spritz of my favorite perfume (Mademoiselle by Chanel), and tucked them into a gift box with a handwritten note. That spring, we were in Harold's.

My rep wasn't trying to be mean, and she wasn't trying to keep me from succeeding. She genuinely believed that she was saving me the trouble of wasting precious resources. But those resources were mine to waste if I wanted to, and even if those samples hadn't been our ticket into Harold's that season, they wouldn't have been wasted. I'd have taken notes on the brands and pieces that made it into the catalog and figured out what we'd been missing from our collection. I'd have followed up with that buyer to share what was new with us and to ask what her own customers were excited about. It wouldn't have been the end of my efforts, just the beginning of a new approach. *No* hurts our ego the most when we think of the other person as a vending machine for our own wants and needs, when we believe that declining a date or RSVPing with regrets for a wedding or not hiring us for the job or not stocking our wares means that we are worthless to one another.

The greatest thing I learned about entrepreneurship was from my mother, who taught me that connection was far more important than any transaction. There was one high-end department store that took us a *long* time to get into. Every time we had a new collection, we'd send our line sheets with some coordinating baked goods: bird cookies for spring, cupcakes decorated with frosting sunflowers for summer. I wrote a personalized, handwritten note with every delivery, and always heard back from her assistant: it wasn't a fit *right* now, they were passing *this* time. She *always* passed, and I *always* got on the phone and asked her assistant for feedback: Was it the colors? The style? What *was* she looking for? I didn't take all of the feedback, but I learned from every conversation, and followed it up with another handwritten thank you note. She'd taken the time to give us her insights, and her time had value. We must have sent this buyer ten packages over the years—had at least ten conversations with her assistant—before she finally called me herself.

She told me that she'd take a meeting with me . . . if I stopped sending all the treats. She'd gained ten pounds, and our deliveries were to blame. Years of *no* were now a *maybe,* one of the biggest opportunities we'd had to date. So we got to work. We put together a presentation, we packed up our samples, and we got on a plane to meet the woman who'd been turning us down for years now. When we finally met, she told us that she'd noticed something in church: the women in the pews around her were all wearing the designs we'd sent her over the years. We joked that it was a sign from God, but in reality it took patience, a genuine curiosity about what she wanted . . . and a helluva lot of sweets. I could have given up after their first *no,* or their fifth, but instead I took it as a learning opportunity. We started in ten stores, then twenty . . . and built a real relationship. We are, to this day, one of the most successful lines that they carry. The lesson: persistence and humility can turn a *no* into a *maybe* . . . and a cupcake never hurts.

Ambition and motivation are great fuel, but not if we forget that people are *people.* Over the years, I've observed that *no* tends to make a person feel less than when they're more focused on the result they want than they are on the human person in front of them. When we focus on the humanity of the person we're interacting with, *no* becomes an invitation to get a little more curious: What does this person need? Want? How could I help *them*?

I've been told *no* in a million different ways in my life and my career:

"We'll pass on this investment opportunity."

"Not right now."

"It's not a good fit."

"Get a life, Stickster."

If I'd taken any of these *no*s as a reflection on my own ability or value, I'd have never gotten out of bed again. But all of these *no*s gave me something I didn't have before: information. Because if you push past the discomfort of your perceived rejection, you can see that the person you're speaking with is giving you an insight into what's important to them, what they need, what they want. Put yourself in their position: when you've said *no,* what was behind it? Saying *no* also gives us valuable information. Nobody likes to feel used, and the quickest way I've found to discern who is here for *me* and who is here for what they think I can do for them is to say *no.* If a *no* breaks the relationship, you never had a relationship, you had a transaction.

I've found that the people most afraid of hearing *no* need to hear it, if only to learn that they can survive it, learn from it, and grow from it. *No* isn't "I hate you." *No* isn't "you're stupid." *No* isn't "give up." It's a big ask, I know, but pay attention to the next time you put yourself out there and hear a *no.* Pause to see where it hits you, what it tells you, and if you're personalizing something that isn't personal. Push beyond your initial discomfort and see if you can spark some curiosity about yourself or the other person. There are plenty of real things to fear in life—brown recluse spiders, global pandemics, the return of low-rise jeans—but *no* is just not one of them.

Eighteen

When It All Falls Apart . . . Again

The business grew exponentially in the wake of every personal tragedy, maybe because I threw myself into work to avoid my feelings and maybe because all of the dominos we'd set up in the years before finally started falling into place. But there's a reason why my first core value is family: it doesn't matter how well things are going at work when your life at home is falling apart. In 2019, I was the twelfth woman in history to be inducted into the Texas Business Hall of Fame . . . and I wasn't there to receive the award. I'd spent months and months anticipating this awards night: my best friends were all going to be there, along with the core group of ladies I'd grown this business with. And even better: I was following in the footsteps of the first woman to be inducted into the TBHF: Mary Kay Ash, whose own business had inspired my mother's journey into entrepreneurship in my childhood. But Dad had suffered a major heart attack, so I got on a plane and handed the acceptance speech duties to my mother. While she stood on a stage in a gorgeous dress, I sat next to his hospital bed with my head on his chest, trying to memorize the beat of his heart. I had—have—no regrets. The choice to live my values—to remain in alignment with who I say I am—was not a choice at all.

When things fall apart, they hardly ever give you a warning. The ground is solid beneath your feet until it isn't, and suddenly you're trapped on that horrible carnival ride where you're pinned to the side of a metal cylinder while the world spins into a blur of colors around you.

It was 2018 and Beck was in eighth grade. Beck has always been the life of every party: as a little kid, he'd greet people with two finger guns while holding his stuffed frog, named Lilla (at age three, he insisted that he would marry Lilla someday . . . he's since changed his mind). From the moment he learned to walk—at *exactly* a year—there was no stopping him. He'd taken his time learning to walk, but from the moment he took those few tentative steps and realized what his legs could do, he wasn't walking ever again . . . he was *running*, and there wasn't a baby gate or a door that could keep him from running off to wherever he wanted to go. He never woke up crying, he woke up laughing, especially on the day when he'd pulled off his diaper and made a painting on the walls and his body . . . using his own poop. He was delighted by his modern art, and John and I were . . . horrified. It was *everywhere*: the walls, the bed, and the baby. John and I divided and conquered, and I picked up Beck with a pair of oven mitts and put him in the bathtub fully clothed. Down the hall I could hear John gagging while he tried to wash the walls.

"I think you got the better deal!" he choked out, and our sweet little devil laughed in glee. It took a good hour to get Beck clean, and a full day for his room to be habitable, and he loved *every* minute of it. Every time we gagged, groaned, or covered our noses, he laughed even harder.

As a kid, Beck is confident and daring, and it makes sense that he loves skiing: you'll find him in the trees, going off jumps, staying out until he's absolutely exhausted and then doing it all again the next day.

It was a day like any other—they always are—and Beck and his cousin were heading out for the very last ski day of the season. This was it, and they wanted to get as much time as they could. I was at my own ski lesson, learning the basic rhythms and movements that Beck seemed to know innately. I was feeling *good*. I made up a new rhyme to help me with my s-turns: *Sashay. All day. Rosé.* And it worked! I was getting it, and most importantly, my instructor thought I was hilarious. I came down the hill for my last run of the day, triumphant and ready for some après ski. Instead, I was greeted by ashen faces and the words I never expected to hear:

"Beck had an accident."

My head filled with static, and my body took over. I threw my poles into the snow and clicked out of my skis and I was off, jumping in my family's car to find our Beck, racing through the winding mountain roads shouting to the ski patrol whether they had a fourteen-year-old boy until my niece called to say that Beck had just arrived at the base with ski patrol. "Go!" I screamed, adrenaline coursing through my veins. In minutes, we pulled up to the hotel, and I jumped out of the moving car and sprinted like a track star toward a group of medics and bystanders, not even noticing that I was still in my ski boots. It had to be Beck, and I had to get to him. I pushed through people who had the audacity to be walking at a leisurely pace, past crowds of happy people enjoying après ski drinks with their friends and family, their laughter ringing in my ears. In the crowd around Beck, I saw my sister and my niece, the gravity of the situation written on their faces. Any form of ski or social etiquette was out the window. I broke through the crowd and screamed, "That's my son!" in a voice I didn't even recognize. I would have charged straight through the crowd but I was stopped by a young paramedic, who grabbed me by the shoulders and looked me in my tear-filled eyes.

"I want you to be with your son," he said slowly, "but he's seriously injured. And you need to get it together. He needs calm energy right now." I looked at myself through his eyes: my face was red and my mascara was streaking down my cheeks, my breath was ragged and my voice so choked I couldn't even speak. Again, *I was wearing ski boots instead of real shoes.* He kept his eyes on mine, and I felt a cool wash through me. My sister hugged me close, and my niece slipped off her winter boots and gave them to me.

"I can do that," I said. "I'll do that." The paramedic took me by the arm, and we stepped through the ski patrol and paramedics toward Beck, and I saw my wild, wonderful boy laying small and broken on a gurney in front of me.

"Hi, baby. I love you," I whispered, kissing his cold cheek.

"I love you, Mom." His voice was a whisper, but he squeezed my hand. I don't know how we got into the ambulance, only that I wanted the driver to *rush*, to get my kid to the hospital as fast as humanly possible. But instead we crept down back roads; his injury was so severe they couldn't risk a sudden stop or any bumps. A blanket covered his body, but in the near silent crawl to the hospital the details were whispered to me. Beck had planned to meet his cousin at the bottom of the mountain, and never showed up. He'd been in the trees—in his element—when he'd skied straight over a thirty-foot drop he didn't know was there. He could have plummeted to his death, but he was caught in a tree, where his right leg wrenched behind him, snapping his femur clean in two. When he came to, he thought he was dead. The goggles and helmet had covered his eyes, and all he could hear was the faint ringing of music from the AirPods that had been jammed into his ears with the impact. There was nobody else around, and he hung there, screaming in pain, for thirty minutes that felt like thirty hours. His phone had broken in his back pocket, but he was able to answer a call from his cousin using Siri and his AirPods.

"I had an accident, and I'm stuck in a tree," he'd said. The shock had made his voice calm and serious, and his cousin had thought Beck was joking. Beck is *always* joking, and the two of them are always pranking each other.

"Funny," his cousin said. "See you at the bottom of the hill." He hung up the phone, and Beck tried to get Siri to call

Cade, me, anyone else. He was losing blood—lots of it—and fighting the urge to relax into the comfort of unconsciousness.

———

The ER in the local hospital is small. Even though the doctor tells me that they've given Beck a drug strong enough to make sure he won't remember this pain, they haven't given me anything, and the scream that I hear echoing through the hallway punctures the part of me that's compartmentalized this day moment by moment. That's my son, in agony, after surviving the pain and terror of facing his own mortality alone. The doctor tells me that Beck's break was so clean it looks like a saw went through his bone and that Beck has developed compartment syndrome, a condition where pressure builds up from internal bleeding and swelling in the tissue, risking muscle loss and nerve damage. The doctors tell me that Beck will be disoriented when he comes to, a combination of the shock and the blood loss and the medications he's been given to manage his pain. I watch as he swims back up from the dark, his eyes struggling to focus. He tells me that the nurses are going to kill him, that he is riding a tiny bicycle across a tightrope, and that there are miniature TIE fighters trying to shoot lasers at his leg.

"Okay, honey," I say, smoothing his hair. Whatever he is on, I want some. I want to be anywhere but here, in this reality. The doctor tells me that the femur is the worst bone to break and that the bottom line is that Beck could lose his leg. The words hang in the air between us like a ghost. Beck can live without a leg, but I cannot live without Beck. I tell the doctors to do whatever it takes to ease his pain and save his leg, and I call our family to tell them that Beck is going to be okay, though I don't know what *okay* means in this new context. I believe it, though: he'll be okay. He has to be.

Twenty-eight days. That's how long Beck and I lived in the hospital in Colorado, while he underwent two blood transfusions and eight surgeries to repair the muscle in his leg. His blood transfusions turned him into a human fish tank, pulling out the old blood and pumping in the new. They had to keep his wound open, and every two days they put him fully under to see if the muscle was alive. If it was, they closed the wound a bit. Before each surgery, he was forced to fast from food *and* water, which is torture in the dry mountain air. His tongue turned to a rock in his mouth, and when he begged and cried for water, I was allowed to swab a wet sponge through his thirsty mouth. Every time he went under before a surgery, they reminded us that he could wake up without that leg.

Day by day, we sat in his room, tubes of blood flowing in and out of his body, and we hoped against hope that his body was healing. The indomitable Beck I'd known for fourteen years had retreated somewhere inside himself, so I brought enough optimism and energy for the both of us. I brought his favorite things into the room—blankets, pillows, photos of our family—and made it feel as much like home as a hospital room can. I brought in a TV, a PlayStation, and a media cart to store it on, so he could play video games with his friends back in Texas. We FaceTimed his brothers every day to catch up on their lives back at home. When I needed to cry, I stepped into the hallway and reapplied my makeup before I stepped back in, so he never had to see my own pain and fear. I could not—would not—leave his side, not even when John came to relieve me. I would leave to take a shower and come right back to sleep on the chair in the corner of the room. When our annual company meeting arrived—a huge event for over five hundred employees—I refused to go. I've told every employee that family comes first, and I mean it. The meeting went on with a cardboard cutout of me onstage.

My brain has committed every moment of those twenty-eight days to long-term memory. I will never forget the way Beck's eyes flinched with pain when the nurses changed his dressings, how the pink slowly returned to his gray face after his first blood transfusion like a black-and-white photo being tinted with color, or how he'd wake from the anesthesia and rip back the blankets to see if his leg was still there. His bravery and tenacity were contagious, and when the doctors told him he was cleared to go home, his cheers lit up the entire room. He didn't care that he was only eighty-seven pounds, that he would have to stay in a wheelchair; he only heard that his leg was saved, and that he got to go home. We donated that TV and PlayStation to the hospital for the next child who needed it, and I told them to call me directly should they ever need another one.

Beck's discharge from the hospital was a critical step in his recovery, but he was far from better. He was a fiercely independent, highly driven eighth grader who now relied on his mom for *everything*. His classmates had come back from winter break and moved on with academics and sports and friendships, and he'd been frozen in place in a bed in Colorado. I wanted to keep him in a glass box where nothing could hurt him ever again, but Beck had other ideas.

"Mom," he said firmly one day, as I checked in on the assignments his teacher had emailed him, "I need to go back to school." Back to school? In person? Out in a world where a kid in the hallway could bump his healing leg with a backpack? Was he *kidding*? He was not. And when Beck Scott wants something, it's best not to get in the way (wonder where he got that from). So, just like I did nine years before when he enrolled in kindergarten, I packed his backpack and drove up to the drop-off line and considered just peeling out and taking him back home. But there were his teachers, his principal, and his friends, smiling and cheering and welcoming him back to his real life.

"We've got him, Kendra," his principal said to me when I started to repeat his medication schedule for the fifth time. "We've got him." Still, I sat in my car and watched as they wheeled him off to class, my heart thumping behind my ribs. They *did* have him. Just like my friends, colleagues, and family had me. Beck was held by a community of friends and family and strangers turned friends whose love saved his life, not just his leg. That skier—the one who *thought* they heard a cry for help? They'd notified the lift operator, who called the ski patrol. But that lift operator didn't *just* call the ski patrol. His shift was ending, and he headed out toward where the skier had heard those cries. He walked in snow up to his chest until he saw Beck—alone and afraid and in shock—and told him he wasn't alone. It took Beck a few days to remember the name of the man who hiked through the snow to find him. David? Daniel? Damon? His name was Damian, and though the shock had kept Beck from truly comprehending the severity of his injury, it was obvious to Damian that this was serious. Beck's body hung like a rag doll in the tree, in a position so unnatural it had to be horrifying. But Damian didn't panic, and he didn't show his fear to Beck. He knew that the ski patrol was still a ways away, so this young man in his twenties made sure my son knew that he wasn't alone. He asked him about school, about his friends, sports. He offered Beck comfort and calm in the darkest, most frightening time in his life, and as soon as I learned that he existed I had to find him. I needed to thank him, to hug him, to let him know that his kindness was extraordinary in the truest sense, that it made a difference in this world.

When he stepped into the hospital room, it was like seeing a long-lost family member. Like any hero, Damian insisted that he was just doing what anyone would do, but he was wrong: it takes an astounding sense of our shared humanity to risk your own comfort and safety for a stranger. In the parking lot, watching Beck leave my side for the first time in months, I remembered Damian and let myself breathe. Beck's got this.

We want our children to learn and grow, but we never want them to have to learn a lesson this hard or this violent. Months after he went back to school, Beck was ready to begin walking on his own again. The first time we watched him take those steps as a baby, we'd safety-proofed the entire house. There were soft covers on the corner of every table and piece of furniture, and John and I had hovered beside him as though he could break his little butt on the carpeting. This time was even more nerve-wracking. He'd been working for months with physical and occupational therapists to regain enough strength to stand, and they braced him with harnesses while he held two parallel bars and attempted to put one foot in front of the other. I've watched Beck bomb down mountains and score touchdowns in flag football and round the bases for a home run. I've watched him shoot free throws for hours and dribble a soccer ball up and down the field tirelessly. But watching him do the ordinary act of walking without any assistance, I cheered like I'd just watched him win the Super Bowl, the Olympics, and the World Series.

A year later, when Beck is a high school freshman who can walk into school without any help and I've even relaxed enough to let his friends drive him to school, Cade calls me. I'm backstage at SXSW with Maria Shriver, preparing for an interview about entrepreneurship. I assume I'll be answering a question about dinner or screen time for their little brother, Grey, but I can tell by the way Cade says "mom" that something is wrong.

"It's Beck," he says, his voice breaking. "We think he broke his leg again."

My head swims. Broke his *leg*? What was he *doing*? How could this happen!

"Mom," he sighs, "he was just walking across the living room."

It had been two weeks since the doctor took the metal plates out of Beck's leg, and Beck had been feeling better than he had since the accident. The doctor had cleared him to play sports, which felt too good to be true. John took the phone and told me that they were getting in the ambulance, and he'd see me there. They were forty minutes from the hospital, but I was much closer, and the interview was scheduled to start in two minutes. I told Maria what happened—she got it, she's a mom—and that I could do twenty-five minutes, no Q&A. For twenty-five minutes, I was brilliant and insightful and inspiring, while my heart in my chest was fluttering in fear. I barely took time to register the applause when our conversation finished and raced out the side door and kicked off my heels, sprinting from backstage to my car, taking five flights of stairs because the elevator was too slow. My driver, Ceasar—yes, of Ceasar's Car Wash—was surprised to see me this soon, but he hit the gas and threw on his flashers, doing whatever it took to get me to my son safely. I got to the hospital five minutes after the ambulance, running into the emergency room and shouting, "Beck Scott! I'm here for Beck Scott!"

Beck's leg had re-broken, and when the doctor showed us the X-ray, everything was different: the break wasn't clean, the bone broke in spiral. He hadn't been breaking the rules and skiing out of bounds, he'd just been walking across the living room to pick up his little sister. He'd just been laughing and joking with Cade and John like his old self, and when they heard him scream, they thought he was joking. But he wasn't, and the Beck in front of us was different from the Beck we saw a month ago, or a year ago. He wasn't sad or scared, like he was back in Colorado. He wasn't frustrated like he was before the doctor took out his plates and cleared him for sports again. He was *mad*. "Mom," he shouted, "why does this keep happening to me?"

Trying to force "perspective" on a person who is suffering is useless and unkind.

I have wondered this, and you likely have, too. Maybe you even got to scream it at the top of your lungs and had someone there to make sense of whatever senseless thing had brought you to your knees. But in this moment, there's no good answer to this question. The scientific, medical reason why Beck's leg re-broke is not a good enough answer when the doctors are telling him that he needs to go back to square one, back to that wheelchair, back to crutches. There's no good spiritual reason either. Bad things happen to good people, and good things happen to them, too. Trying to force "perspective" on a person who is suffering is useless and unkind; his perspective—that he's a high school freshman, the bottom of the social food chain, and now he has to be markedly different from his classmates, put his athletics and academics on the back burner and focus on healing—is real and it's valid. He is not okay, and that's okay.

For months after his accident, I was not either. Once the shock wore off, I was gripped by fear and helplessness; with any of the boys out of my sight, my heart would suddenly clench with the realization that *something could be wrong.* I'd check their breathing in the middle of the night—fine when you have a newborn, less fine when your oldest is in high school—and find myself suddenly unable to breathe should I see a missed call from any of them. I might be in a meeting about our supply chain, and then suddenly be ripped from my body and the present moment and into a darker world in my imagination. I'd see Beck's open flesh on the hospital bed, gruesome details from the accident I'd never even seen myself. I'd wake up in the middle of the night choking for air, panicking and unable to orient myself, certain that something was Very Wrong.

Something was very wrong, but I needed the help of professionals to see it and to heal it. Beck was suffering from post-traumatic stress disorder, which I could understand. But I learned that PTSD wasn't just for the person who experienced the traumatic injury, but for those who were affected by it. It was not just about what I experienced, but *how* I experienced it. That loss of control with Beck's accident had triggered the loss of control I'd felt so many times in my life: with losing my grandpa, with Rob, with Holley, with the divorces and the market crash. To sort through all of the emotional detritus in my brain—to re-train my nervous system to stop simply reacting and to recognize a *feeling* vs. a real emergency—took months. It was a process like any other, painful and slow but ultimately healing. Beck would get there, too. He'd get back on his feet and work through his own trauma. But it takes *time* to renew your sense of hope when you're faced with hopelessness; it takes time for the window of perspective to widen, and the emotional healing took longer than the physical. Years from that moment in the hospital room, he'd be inviting me on daylong hikes and chasing his little brother around the front yard. He'd be doing yoga with me in the living room and starting his own business before he even got a high school diploma. But neither of us knew that yet. We only knew that ahead of him was more work, and more pain.

Hopelessness is the hardest thing. He had lost so much hope. There was such a small window of perspective. It would take so much work—but that's his story to tell. There were years of him waking up from nightmares of falling. Physical healing and emotional healing are different.

"Why does this keep happening to me?"

There is no answer to this question, so I tell him the truth: I don't know why this keeps happening to him. What I do know is that life is tough, and so is he. And that it's okay for him to be angry, to be scared, to hate that this is happening, that when he feels his fire dimming, we will be here to stoke the flames for him. Watching my son struggle physically and mentally and come out thriving inspired me to be more open and honest. My insistence on being the Super Mom who is always upbeat and positive was because we don't *want* our kids to see our suffering. And while we never want our kids to carry our adult burdens, it's okay for our kids to know that our lives are not always perfect, that we experience a full range of human emotions. I didn't realize that part of my positivity had made my boys feel like they always had to be doing okay. Hiding my tears from my kids had made them feel like they had to hide theirs. Our relationships have deepened since the accident because those shiny, happy walls I didn't know I'd built up came crumbling down. I remind him that it's okay for him to be hurting.

I remind him of his first steps, and his second first steps, and of Damian, walking through chest-high snow to pull him to safety. I remind him that the kindness he has put into the world has come back to him before, and it will again. That when things fall apart, something else will fall together. I am, I know, reminding myself. That there is good in the world, and when we have trouble seeing it, we can make some ourselves.

Nineteen

Yellow-Colored Glasses

R ose-colored glasses are overrated. I prefer yellow-colored glasses, because no offense to people who love pink, but yellow makes even a gray day seem brighter. Of course, things aren't *always* bright and cheerful, and that fall I took into the gulch was a literal wake-up call, shaking me by the shoulders and waking me up. In the months that followed that accident, I spent months with my life coach trying to get back my yellow-colored glasses.

But shifting your perspective isn't as easy as just *deciding* you feel a different way, it's truly sitting with the feelings you have. It's acknowledging and respecting where you are so that you can move forward, and I . . . didn't want to do that! Because what I was feeling was *terrible*. It was like an ice cream sundae of bad. To start, I had the terror of my father's precarious health, and the stark realization that there is no amount of money or success that can protect you from the frailties of the human body. Sprinkled on top of this were my own health issues and some deep interpersonal wounds and—the cherry on top—the Mom Guilt. We all have it at some point, I know, but this is the worst it's ever been. Because I was divorced . . . *again*. The bigger boys had already been through this, but Grey had not, and watching his little brain and heart process what it meant for his parents to no longer be together was excruciating. It *would* be okay—I thought—but in the moment it was not.

Shifting your perspective isn't as easy as just deciding you feel a different way, it's truly sitting with the feelings you have. It's acknowledging and respecting where you are so that you can move forward.

The psychologist Susan David wrote that "our emotions are data. Our emotions contain flashing lights to things that we care about."[1] The feelings that I'm a bad mom, that fear for my father, the terror of the world spinning out of control . . . they led me back to my core values. I value family, presence, kindness, joy. I value *people*, and giving what I can to make people feel safe and seen. My feelings weren't something that needed fixing, they *needed* feeling. I knew that I would not always feel this way, I would not always be here in this moment. Someday, the wounds I was tending to would heal, and the sting would be nothing but a scar. I could let it hurt in the moment and slip on my yellow-colored glasses to look ahead to a brighter future.

That Vivid Visions exercise I did with Cameron back in EO was a powerful way to envision the kind of future I wanted for the company. Everything I'd written out had become true, not because I worked some magic spell but because I knew exactly what I was working toward, and so did my team. Like most people, the chaos of 2020 had put me into a tornado of shifting needs and demands; even with solid core values I felt like my internal compass was constantly trying to find its way North. I'd stepped back from running the company as the CEO and into a role as chairwoman, owner, and designer. Kendra Scott the company has a board of directors and a leadership team and thousands of employees to keep it on track, and I trusted fully in the team I'd built to lead the company into the future based on our core values. I had—in this moment—myself, my friends, and my boys. Cade and Beck were now teenagers, not the little kids they were when I was building the company. So I revisited that Vivid Visions exercise with my life coach, Katie, and applied it to my personal life. I sat in the sunniest corner of my living room with a fresh notebook and I set a vision for my life in the next three years.

I was born and raised in the Midwest, but after three decades here in Texas, I'm definitely a Texan, and I felt myself pulled toward land and nature, open skies and a more open schedule. I still love my glam, but I'm happiest when I'm on a hike, or digging in dirt, or on the back of a horse. I thought about spreading joy and creating opportunity, and what I could do to grow the Kendra Scott Women's Entrepreneurial Leadership Institute at UT. If I wasn't running the day-to-day operations of the company, I would have time to actually teach a course every semester. I'd have time to write a book! I

but those hours are our most precious resource. When we add up the hours we thought we *had* to give, we have entire days and weeks of our life that we spent unwillingly. *Ick*.

I went through my calendar with a fine-tooth comb and cleared the things I didn't really *need* to do. There were meetings that the team could handle without me, events that I *wanted* to attend but meant time away from the boys, and fancy parties that just didn't sound as good as a Friday night in the basement listening to Willie Nelson with my friends. I left space—in my calendar, in my plans—and my days began to fill with the kinds of things that filled me up until I was spilling over with the joy and optimism and energy I'd always had so effortlessly.

I was *me* again.

The power of this exercise is that it isn't prescriptive. There isn't a person telling you what to do or how to do it, there is just time spent with your mind, your heart, and a pen and paper. This exercise isn't about traditional accomplishments, unless you really want it to be. The Great Resignation has taught a lot of people that they don't need to keep climbing, and that it's more than okay to stop and enjoy the view from where they are. It's okay to provide for your family *and* provide for yourself, to have work that fulfills you but isn't the *only* thing fulfilling you. It's okay to raise the bar *and* appreciate where you are. Before you start, try to clear your mind of what you think other people expect of you, or what you assume is the next step you *have* to take. The world does not need a billion copies of me, or of any prototype you have for success. The world needs you, pursuing your dreams, living the life you imagine for yourself. What emerges—and what you do with it—is entirely up to you.

Here are some of the prompts I've used. The rules are the same as Cameron's: don't worry about the how, just write it as if it's what's true three years from now. Put on your yellow-colored glasses. Ready? Go.

Describe where you live: Maybe you have a renovated kitchen or a new bed frame, and maybe your house is exactly the same . . . but decluttered and tidy. Are you in the same city you live in now, or have you moved to the place you always dreamed about? Are there busy city streets or palm trees waving in the sky? Don't think about *how* you got there, just imagine that you're there.

Describe your day, in as much detail as you can: When you wake up in the morning, what do you see? Feel? What's the first thing you do? Maybe it's ten minutes of yoga, or reading. Maybe it's heading straight for the coffee machine and scrolling your phone. What do you put on in the morning, and how does it feel? What do you eat? What happens as your day unfolds, and how does it feel? Are you crushing it at work, or spending hours in the garden?

Who is in your life? Are you currently partnered? Write about what your partnership is like in its ideal form. Forget whatever baggage you're currently carrying and think only about the vision you're creating.

What qualities do you bring out in each other, what do your dates look like?

If you're currently single, write out who your ideal partner is: what do they like, what do they like about *you*? What makes them laugh? What do they care about? Where do they fit into the vision you've already created: are they the center of this world, or a supporting character? Get as specific as you can, not with the expectation that you'll meet a person who checks all of these boxes, but with the expectation that when you know what you *do* want, you won't waste time on what you *don't*.

Are you surrounded by a large group of acquaintances or a tight group of friends? Who are you spending your time with, and how does this time *feel* to you? What do these relationships give you, and what do they bring out in you?

What does your family—of origin and creation—look and feel like? Who sits at your dinner table every night, and who is your emergency contact?

Pay attention to the relationships that you cultivate, and the ones that have dissolved. We sometimes make decisions based on how other people will feel about them, but again, this is your vision, not theirs, so you don't need to get into the details of what has happened, or how they will react . . . just *your* ideal scenario.

Think of your Big Life Moments: How do you spend your birthdays? Holidays? Who is there with you and how does it feel to you? Do you go all out or keep it small and intimate?

Who can help you bring this vision to life? What kind of help do you need? How will you ask for it?

The power of this exercise is that it isn't prescriptive. There isn't a person telling you what to do or how to do it, there is just time spent with your mind, your heart, and a pen and paper.

That last question is important. It's hard sometimes to be honest about what we want: if we say it out loud, people will *know*! They'll know that we're actually striving for something and—even worse!—they'll know if we don't find it or achieve it. But if we open up about what we want and need, if we shout it out to everyone we love and trust, something magical can happen. Because life is a group project: individuals thrive when they have strong relationships and strong communities holding them up. Whatever your vision, you will need other people to help bring it to life. When I'd needed a COO to step in and do all of the things that I didn't want to do and wasn't good at, I'd told anyone who would listen what our company needed to grow. I had to be honest about what we didn't have—what *I* didn't have—and trust that this vulnerability would pay off. It did. We found Lon, who never in a million years would have been searching through job boards looking for a job with a little jewelry startup in Texas.

When you have the vision, you can start to build the map. When you know that you want to live near the beach, you stop looking for jobs in the mountains. When you know that you want friendships based on trust and respect, you stop spending time with people who make you feel small and insecure. When you know you want to foster dogs, you stop renting apartments with a no-pet policy. When you know you want to run a marathon in three years, you start with a jog around the block. When you hit a detour—when your choices are not aligned with your values and your vision—you'll *feel* it, and as humans we've been given an unbelievable gift of intuition. You can feel when something is and isn't right. The more you listen to it, the stronger it gets.

*If we open up about what we want and
need, if we shout it out to everyone we love
and trust, something magical can happen.*

Not all of life is within our control, and the visions we create for our lives do not all come true. The point of this isn't to create an unrealistic standard for yourself, but to create the time and space for you to see your life and your world as optimistically as possible. Life is filled with people and situations dedicated to telling you who you are and what you can and cannot do. Our own brains are often our worst critics. I am not going to tell you that things won't go wrong if you *just think hard enough*, but I'd like to see you give yourself a gift: a bit of time to set aside what could go wrong and imagine everything that could go *right*, to let go of what is and imagine what could be. Your vision does not exist to impress anyone else. It exists to inspire you, to drive you, a bright spot to focus on when the darkness comes creeping in along the edges. My vision brought me back to the truest version of myself, one that had felt lost to me for a time.

Whatever emerges from these pages, it is *you*. These are your thoughts, your dreams, your vision. You are the author and the hero of your own story, and regardless of whether you're reaching for a big dream or paring down to a simpler vision, you are also worth loving and celebrating just as you are right now. Because who and where you are right now is no small thing. You have survived every one of your worst days, have kept breathing after moments that knocked the wind out of you. You are the culmination of everything that you have ever been through: every broken heart, every big dream, every laugh, and every tear. None of it was wasted, and it never is.

The dark will come again, and when it does, we will do our best to shine the light for one another. Light itself is made up of a spectrum of colors; life, for all of us, is a spectrum of experiences, stories, moments of impact and doubt and triumph. On your darkest days, I hope you remember that light inside of you, that everything you've been through can be used to make something new, something valuable, and something that shines as bright as you do.

ACKNOWLEDGMENTS

f I were to list all the people who made it possible for me to get to this moment . . . I'd need a whole other book. I am the sum of all my experiences and the people who have loved me along the way. I am forever grateful to my mother, my father, and Rob for their love and guidance, to Aunt Jo Ann for the inspiration to dream big, and to my big sisters and little brothers for their love and support.

My family is not just the branches on my family tree, but the entire Kendra Scott organization. I am so proud of our people and our culture, and grateful to share this dream with a group of people who are passionate about our mission to truly spread joy in the world. To the Super Seven, thank you for never being afraid to wear all sorts of hats during our growth and always doing it with a smile! To our amazing CEO, Tom, I am truly grateful to work beside you every day.

I'm eternally grateful to have a group of friends like no other, my Señoras, you know who you are. I couldn't do life without you amazing women! Being a mom is the best job in the world, and I couldn't do it without the big, blended group of kids and dogs I come home to every day. Cade, Beck, Grey, Anni, Aili, and Tommy . . . I love you all to the moon and back!

Duke is, of course, the love of my life, but Thomas is a close second. I love you so much.

I couldn't have written this book without my fantastic agent, Cait Hoyt, my amazing editor, Daisy Hutton, and the team of people who keep me on track every day and are more than just work colleagues but family: Tyler, Kevin, Kathy, Kelly.

I'm grateful for all my mentors and advisers, all of my colleagues, every single customer, and you, the reader . . . I am forever honored to be a part of your lives.

NOTES

CHAPTER 4: 9 TO 5

1. https://www.mckinsey.com/featured-insights/diversity-and-inclusion/women-in-the-workplace#.

2. https://www.spglobal.com/marketintelligence/en/news-insights/research/changepays-there-were-more-male-ceos-named-john-than-female-ceos.

3. https://www.nytimes.com/2021/02/18/us/politics/women-pandemic-harris.html#:~:text=Trillion%20Economic%20Plan-,2.5%20Million%20Women%20Left%20the%20Work%20Force%20During%20the%20Pandemic,for%20women%20workers%20at%20risk.%E2%80%9D.

CHAPTER 9: SHAKING THE SNOW GLOBE

1. https://www.entrepreneur.com/article/361350.

2. https://www.inc.com/magazine/20080801/how-we-did-it-the-blue-man-group.html.

CHAPTER 12: WE DO GOOD

1. https://www2.deloitte.com/content/dam/insights/us/articles/2020-global-marketing-trends/DI_2020%20Global%20Marketing%20Trends.pdf.

CHAPTER 19: YELLOW-COLORED GLASSES

1. https://www.ted.com/talks/susan_david_the_gift_and_power_of_emotional_courage/transcript?language=en.

CHAPTER 1: IN THE ROUGH

1. "I'm out of that gulch—literally and figuratively—and I know that someday, I could fall back in. And when that happens, I *have* to ask for help. The people who love me came running to the rescue. They heard me when nobody else did, and they'd do it again. I never want to forget that, and I want to keep my own ear trained to hear the cries for help around me."

   Q: *Have you ever found yourself in a figurative gulch? What was that experience like? Who are the people who helped you out of it?*

2. "I'm tired of women pretending like their work is effortless, their success a fluke, that the success of another woman is a ding against them instead of a point for *all* of us."

   Q: *As a woman, have you ever felt like you had to pretend you had everything together? What were some of the lasting effects of that pressure?*

3. "Here's the promise I'd like to see us make for one another: that when we're down, we'll reach out for help. That when we're up, we'll reach back and offer a hand."

   Q: *Discuss the importance of this mutual giving and receiving of help.*

CHAPTER 2: PROUD TO BE A COAL MINER'S GRANDDAUGHTER

1. "I imagined myself growing up to be just like Jo Ann, surrounded by beauty and style at work and at home, making a life of my own on my own, just like she did."

   Q: *Did you have any influential women in your life early on? Who were they and what kind of impact did they have on you?*

2. "While my mother and her siblings were expected to stay on the farm, my father and his sister were encouraged to go, to dream, to let their roots stabilize them but not immobilize them."

Q: *Discuss your "roots." Where did you come from? Were you encouraged to explore your passions and interests, or were you expected to follow in your family's footsteps?*

3. "The best lessons you learn are the ones you never realize are being taught to you."

Q: *What is one lesson you've held on to throughout your life, but at the time didn't even realize was being taught to you?*

CHAPTER 3: FAMILY FIRST

1. "We hardly ever know what moments and memories will become building blocks for who we are. Change is the same way: in the moment, do we never know which choice we make is going to be the one that changes everything?"

Q: *What are some building block moments in your own life?*

2. "Growing up, the kind of family you have is the only kind of family you know about, but even if I'd been given a menu of options, I'd have picked being the youngest of four girls."

Q: *How did your place within your family (oldest child, middle child, youngest child, only child) shape your sense of self and your sense of how you fit into the world?*

CHAPTER 4: 9 TO 5

1. "This was the world I longed to inhabit: where women linked arms and moved up the ladder together, where they saw each other not as competition but as comrades."

Q: *Do you see this reality playing out in our world today? Where? If not, why do you think that is?*

2. "Because just like my mother and plenty of women before and after her, many of us have been forced to choose between work and the rest of our lives."

Q: *Have you ever felt pressure to pick between work and "the rest of your life"? If so, how did that make you feel?*

3. "As human beings, our lives are an asset to our careers, not a liability . . . Our experiences outside of work enrich our lives *at* work. They bring perspective and compassion and empathy and *personality* to the workplace."

Q: *Do you agree with this? Why or why not?*

CHAPTER 5: STICKSTER

1. "Every room we step into, whether we're invited or we push our way in, we're stepping into a perception that people have of us: of our capabilities, our value, our worth. It's the easiest thing in the world to believe what people say about you, to let their opinion of you be the deciding factor in whether or not you move forward."

Q: *Talk about a time when people's perceptions of you didn't line up with reality. What was that experience like?*

2. "Whatever people say about you, your business, your dreams . . . there is nobody who knows who you are or what you're capable of more than you do."

Q: *Why is it so important to believe in yourself even when, from the outside, it looks like everything is against you?*

3. "So sing it with me until you believe it: I have confidence in me."

Q: *Do you have any mantras that you repeat to yourself when you're feeling discouraged?*

CHAPTER 6: DETOUR TO DESTINY

1. "You must learn to pivot quickly and adjust to what's happening around you, and to sometimes let go of your ideas of how things should be or what you want."

Q: *What ideas or dreams have you needed to let go of? What was this process like for you, and how did you adjust to your new reality?*

2. "I hated that school, and looking back knowing what I know now about mental health, I'm sure that I was clinically depressed. I knew there was something else out there for me, but I didn't know how to get it."

Q: *Depression in teenagers has reached unprecedented levels in the wake of the pandemic. What about your teenage self do you wish that you and your parents had better understood? How could you use this insight to help younger people grow through their teen years with better self-awareness and improved mental health?*

3. "For a lot of people, college feels mandatory: it's something our parents expected of us, especially if they didn't get the opportunity to go themselves. For generations, we've been told that it's the path to success, that without it, we'll end up going nowhere fast."

Q: *Kendra felt pressure to go to college, even though she knew, somewhere deep down, that it was not right for her. What major decisions in your life have you felt pressured into because it was perceived to be the "right thing to do"?*

CHAPTER 7: YOU DO GOOD

1. "I realized very quickly the first lesson of entrepreneurship: you can't be in it for the money."

Q: *What does Kendra mean by this statement? How can it apply in every aspect of our choices about our career and our life's purpose?*

2. "I was doing good, I would do good. This—these words—were my life's purpose."

Q: *What does doing good look like for you relative to your own life's purpose?*

3. "Closing a business is even harder than opening one. There's no dream on the horizon to run toward, just a finish line where the ribbon has already been cut and the crowds have gone home, like coming in dead last in a race against yourself."

Q: *What have you learned through your own life experiences about dealing with loss and disappointment when you can't see the reason or the next step on the horizon?*

CHAPTER 8: BEHIND EVERY STRONG WOMAN

1. "All women are expected to be superheroes: to do it all, look good doing it, and assure you *it was no problem, really!* I hate this lie; I hate what it does to us, and how it tears us apart from each other by creating and perpetuating a false standard that literally none of us can live up to."

    Q: *How has the lie of perfection had an impact on your decisions, on your mental and physical health, on your relationships?*

2. "It felt like the perfect life I'd worked so hard to create had become a snow globe that the universe had shaken without my permission. I was stuck in place while the pieces of my life I thought had been immovable were swirling around me."

    Q: *Talk about a time in your life when you felt the way Kendra describes in this statement. How did you get through that time? What did your life look like on the other side?*

3. "Behind every successful woman is a whole community of people helping her, supporting her, reassuring her."

    Q: *Has community been an important support system in your life? If yes, how? If not, why?*

CHAPTER 9: SHAKING THE SNOW GLOBE

1. "Life is hard for everyone, and it's certainly not fair."

    Q: *Throughout the book, including this chapter, Kendra discusses instance after instance where the timing of her ventures seemed to be all wrong—where she had doors slammed in her face that then allowed other doors to open. Can you think of a time in your life when what seemed like terrible timing actually turned out to be a gift in disguise?*

2. "What I saw in the midst of this chaos was that relationships had been the key to my success so far."

    Q: *Kendra's revelation about the importance of relationships to success allowed her to innovate and to extend her business through connecting directly with* consumers, thereby digging the business out of the Great Recession. Can you think of a time in your own life when the power of relationships has allowed you to overcome a major obstacle?

3. "The optimist in me is going to tell you that fear is not your enemy, but your friend. Every moment of dramatic, positive forward change in my life has come from fear."

Q: Talk about a time in your life when fear compelled you toward dramatic, positive change.

CHAPTER 10: THE BILLION-DOLLAR SEAT

1. "The only way to navigate uncharted territory is to find people who have been there before."

Q. In this chapter, Kendra discusses the importance of proactively seeking out mentors to help you chart a path to new things. Talk about an important mentor in your life and how that person helped you to move forward in your goals and in your life. Do you have a mentor in your life right now? If not, why and what can you do to change that?

2. "One of you is sitting in a billion-dollar seat."

Q: Have you ever sat, figuratively (or literally!), in a billion-dollar seat? Describe how it happened.

CHAPTER 11: WHAT MATTERS TO YOU?

1. "My personal brand and my actual brand aren't all that different. Because a brand is not just the perfect logo or the right color (although those are crucial elements, and Cheryl *nailed* it on both counts). A brand is what you do and why you do it, a reflection on the people who created it and who support it."

Q: What is your personal brand? How does it reflect who you are and what you believe in?

2. "When I'm asked for branding advice—and sometimes even when I'm not—I tell people to be honest. To be who they are. Anyone can sniff out a phony, and nobody likes a faker. A lot of

the people you see posting on Instagram and talking about their personal brand are faking it."

Q: *What are some of the negative consequences of perfection/comparison culture in your own life or in the life of someone you love? Think of a new way that you can apply the values of honesty and authenticity in your own life.*

3. "Being clear on your core values is like lining up the foundation of who you are."

Q: *Take a moment to think about and record your core values. Then take a moment to consider how these values have shaped your life and decisions so far, and how they might shape specific decisions you are making or will be making about your future.*

CHAPTER 12: WE DO GOOD

1. "I'd been told by an investor once that artists didn't make good businesspeople because we were too concerned with how things looked to pay attention to how they worked. I thought of him every time we shipped an order or collected an invoice."

Q: *Are there any words of advice or wisdom that you've been given and have believed that need to be questioned and discarded or amended? How would it change your way of thinking and doing things if you let go of these well-intentioned untruths?*

2. "Success cannot just be limited to the bottom line. Very few people are energized by or inspired to work with companies whose only purpose is growth."

Q: *How can this principle be applied directly in your life— whether it's your business, your family, your friendships and relationships, or your goals?*

3. "Whatever you can give has immense value, no matter the dollar value attached to it. Give what you can, when you can, and know that all of it counts, all of it matters."

Q: *Think of at least one new way that you could be giving—whether it be financially, your time, or your skills. What would it take to add this new activity to your life and schedule?*

CHAPTER 13: AVERAGE FAMILY

1. "My parents' divorce was painful for me, but spending time with my dad in our little condo—or with my mom in Chicago—didn't feel broken. It felt normal. It wasn't what I chose, but it *was* what I had."

    Q: *Think of an extremely difficult circumstance in your life. Now, think about not what you lost through that circumstance but rather what was left for you to continue to build your life around. Consider how that difficult circumstance shaped your core values and your sense of self. Are there stories you are believing about your past circumstances that you need to let go of in order to embrace the best of what life has coming your way?*

2. "To show up ready and willing to brave the risk of heartbreak when your best laid plans have been decimated is gutsy and admirable."

    Q: *Kendra makes the above statement in reference to the aftermath of a divorce. Is there a situation in your life that has caused you to shy away from risking disappointment or heartbreak? What would it take for you to overcome these fears and take this risk again?*

3. "Not everyone has a family of origin that makes them feel safe and loved . . . As children, there's nothing we can do about the family we're given."

    Q: *Are there issues or wounds from your family of origin that haunt you or hold you back from living your fullest life? If so, what steps could you take that might diminish the power that these experiences have over your life?*

CHAPTER 14: OWN IT

1. "We tell our kids that 'everybody makes mistakes,' but do we want to be a part of that everybody?"

   Q: *Take a moment to reflect on your own relationship with failure. Is it something that you fear, or is it something that you see as an inevitable part of growth?*

2. "You're only as good as the people you get advice from."

   Q: *Think about a piece of advice you've been given that has been helpful to you in your life so far on repeated occasions.*

3. "To move on from any mistake or failure, we must be able to own it. When we avoid taking responsibility for our choices, our actions, and what didn't work, shame creeps in and takes root. I once heard that when you point the finger, there are three more pointing back at you."

   Q: *Think about a mistake or failure that has been extremely difficult for you to take responsibility for. What would it mean for you to take ownership of it? How could your life improve if you do the hard work of taking this step?*

CHAPTER 15: HITTING THE FLOOR

1. "Mental health care was simply not a part of the conversation in 1980s Kenosha, Wisconsin. I'd undergone a seriously traumatic event, and I couldn't think, couldn't sleep, couldn't speak."

   Q: *Kendra writes the above passage in reference to losing her grandfather and the guilt that she felt for not being home with him when he died. Have you suffered a trauma that deeply affected you and for which you are still carrying guilt and shame? What would it take for you to release those feelings, and how are those feelings holding you back from living your best life?*

2. "I'm a fixer: present me with a problem and I'll find ten new ways to solve it, and twenty more if the first ten don't work out. But not everything in life can be solved."

> Q: *What do you do when you encounter problems that you are not able to fix? What resources do you draw upon? Where else might you be able to go for support and help through such seasons?*

3. "To me, that's the crux of finding meaning: moving beyond your own experience and into the way your experience connects you to the world."

> Q: *Think about a specific time in your own life when your personal suffering allowed you to connect more meaningfully with the people around you.*

CHAPTER 16: HOW TO FIGHT

1. "Grown-ups know that hurt people hurt people, that every bully has a backstory that usually involves their own emotional or physical abuse."

> Q: *The kind of middle school bullying that Kendra talks about is pretty easy to spot, but have you ever been the victim of bullying as an adult? How did you handle it?*

2. "The urge to defend ourselves against hateful people is strong and primal; we want people to like us, to see us as good . . . But do not let someone else's opinion of you become *your* opinion of you."

> Q: *Think of a situation where you've been forced to defend yourself against people who wanted to take you down. What did you do? How were you able to remain true to who you are while not letting a hater get the best of you?*

3. "My grandfather used to tell me that when you wrestle a pig, you both get dirty...but the pig likes it."

> Q: *Think of a time when you've wrestled a pig. How did it turn out?*

CHAPTER 17: THE POWER OF *NO*

1. "The greatest thing I learned about entrepreneurship was from my mother, who taught me that connection was far more important than any transaction."

    Q: *Can you think of an example of this truth that you experienced personally—either in business or in your personal life?*

2. "If I'd taken any of these *no*s as a reflection on my own ability or value, I'd have never gotten out of bed again. But all of these *no*s gave me something I didn't have before: information."

    Q: *Think about a time in your life when a* no *actually turned into an opportunity—to learn, to grow, to head in another (and better!) direction.*

CHAPTER 18: WHEN IT ALL FALLS APART . . . AGAIN

1. "When things fall apart, they hardly ever give you a warning. The ground is solid beneath your feet until it isn't, and suddenly you're trapped on that horrible carnival ride where you're pinned to the side of a metal cylinder while the world spins into a blur of colors around you."

    Q: *What has been the most disorienting loss you've experienced in your life? How did you get through it?*

2. "Something was very wrong, but I needed the help of professionals to see it and to heal it. Beck was suffering from post-traumatic stress disorder, which I could understand. But I learned that PTSD wasn't just for the person who experienced the traumatic injury, but for those who were affected by it."

    Q: *Have you ever experienced an event so traumatic that you knew you needed the support of a professional to help you heal?*

3. "While we never want our kids to carry our adult burdens, it's okay for our kids to know that our lives are not always perfect, that we experience a full range of human emotions. I didn't

realize that part of my positivity had made my boys feel like they always had to be doing okay."

Q: *Can you think of a time in your life when you tried to protect those you love but your efforts ended up backfiring, creating more pain than protection? How do we know how to walk the line between strength and vulnerability when we encounter suffering?*

CHAPTER 19: YELLOW-COLORED GLASSES

1. "When you have everything you need, you also have to make sure that you want what you have, that you cut back on the things that don't serve you."

   Q: *Have you experienced the kind of culling season that Kendra describes above? If so, what did you let go of that no longer served you?*

2. "If we open up about what we want and need, if we shout it out to everyone we love and trust, something magical can happen."

   Q: *What is something that you either want or need that you may be holding back from putting out into the world? What can you do to overcome this holding back and be vulnerable with others about where you want your life to go?*

3. "Light itself is made up of a spectrum of colors; life, for all of us, is a spectrum of experiences, stories, moments of impact and doubt and triumph."

   Q: *Kendra began and ended this book with a reminder that true joy and beauty are made up of a combination of light and darkness. Has the experience of reading this book changed your perspective on the relationship between pain and joy? How can you apply what you've learned the next time you experience disappointment or even suffering?*

ABOUT THE AUTHOR

*D*esigner, founder, and philanthropist Kendra Scott started her company in 2002, just three months after her first son was born. Her commitment to innovation, quality, and detail has taken her from a small startup to a billion-dollar brand. Kendra was awarded the EY Entrepreneur of the Year National Award in 2017, was inducted into the Texas Business Hall of Fame in 2019, and appeared as the only female guest Shark on Season 12 of ABC's *Shark Tank*. With a passion for empowering the next generation of female leaders, Kendra is currently a Professor of Practice at the Kendra Scott Women's Entrepreneurial Leadership Institute at the University of Texas at Austin. In addition, Kendra is a member of the board of directors for the Breast Cancer Research Foundation and the Council of Fashion Designers of America while she maintains her position as executive chairwoman and chief creative officer of Kendra Scott, LLC. Today, her company continues to operate out of Austin, Texas, where she lives with her family. Visit KendraScott.com for more!